Total Market Takeover®
For Your
Professional Practice

Gordon Van Wechel and Jennine Michael

DEDICATION

To Dr. Joseph A. Michael II, whose memory never fades;
and to Gordon Van Wechel who taught me that happiness and love are not
limited to once in a lifetime.

Jennine Michael

I was blessed early in my business career with three mentors:

Jack Driscoll, who taught me how to analyze a business,
Pastor Steve Hartman, who encouraged me to strive for balance in my life,
and Tom Wilscam, a serial entrepreneur if there ever was one!

My thanks to each of you.

Gordon Van Wechel

CONTENTS

Introduction   i

1   Finding Bedrock   1

2   Reputation Marketing   29

3   Lead Generation Website   59

4   Retargeting   83

5   Pay-Per-Click Advertising   95

6   Real Time Bidding   135

7   Video Marketing   163

8   Appreciation Marketing   185

9   TMT Done For Your   195

10   11 Most Asked Questions   203

Gordon Van Wechel & Jennine Michael

Introduction

When Gordon was in graduate school, one of his professors was fond of saying that whenever we read a book, listen to a speaker, or read an article in an industry magazine, one of the things we should always do is determine the author's bias. What is their frame of reference? Why do they reach the conclusions they want you to accept? How did they choose the data they offer as proof of their position? Are they hoping to sell you something, or convert you to a particular belief?

As you read this book, we are going to save you from struggling with that issue. We will tell you right up front what we believe about marketing and the challenge of being a professional practice owner in today's difficult economic climate. We wish we could claim this as original thought, but it is a statement from a speech by the late Peter Drucker. He said, **"There are only two important activities for a business owner to be involved in: marketing and innovation. Everything else can be delegated."**

Marketing is sharing what your practice does and inspiring people to choose to do business with you. *Innovation* is making sure that your practice is responsive to the changing wants of your clients and patients, and that it is the best it can be. According to

Professor Drucker, these are the only activities that we, as business owners, should be focused on.

We understand how easy it may seem for a university professor to make a statement like that. He likely has never worked sixty-hour weeks, struggled to make payroll, and missed family activities to solve a patient issue. Those of us who have been entrepreneurs know all too well about those times, particularly in the early days of starting a practice.

However, we believe that Professor Drucker was right. As your practice comes out of the initial "survival mode," and as you identify some key people to help you and achieve a degree of stability, your focus as the owner must change if you are to create a sustainable enterprise. Most of us who have started a business have the vision that we are creating an asset—one which, at some time in the future, we can sell or turn over to a good manager and enjoy the fruits of our labor.

To make that happen, we have to transition from working so hard "in" our practice and begin to work "on" our practice. That means we have to step back from making *all* the decisions, in order to focus on innovating our company to be the best it can be. Then, we implement the most effective marketing strategies so that clients can find us.

We have written this book to help you identify several of today's best marketing strategies for a professional practice. These strategies have been proven in "real world" situations with our clients in markets across the country. We call our program "Total Market Takeover®"—a name that evolved as we saw our clients begin to grow their market share as a result of implementing this multi-channel approach.

We will use two terms interchangeably within this book: client and patient. We understand that medical professionals generally refer to their "patients" and other professional practices have "clients." Regardless of which word we use, our intent is to focus on the prospect for your practice.

This is not a book about marketing theory. We are going to share with you exactly what we do when implementing Total Market Takeover® in a practice. We encourage you to take notes and put these strategies to use. At the end of each chapter, we will suggest the next steps you should take if you want to implement that particular strategy into your practice marketing plan.

The back of the book contains information about our company and how to contact us directly. In fact, we are offering readers a free, one-hour opportunity to talk with us about your practice. We encourage you to take us up on that offer.

"But advertising my practice is so, well, unprofessional..."

A long history of controversy surrounds the idea of professionals advertising their services. Late in the nineteenth century, the Minnesota state medical board debated the ethics of advertising by physicians. The Secretary of the Board went so far as to say, "I am opposed to physicians even putting up a sign in their dooryards."

In the 1970s, the State Bar of Arizona suspended two attorneys for newspaper advertising—a case that went all the way to the U.S. Supreme Court. Ultimately, the attorneys' right to advertise was upheld, but the bar association was permitted to "regulate" advertising. It is interesting to note that in 2011, trial attorneys spent $52.6 million with Google AdWords alone. By way of comparison, the Obama 2008 campaign, considered by many to be an example of how to use social media correctly, spent just $16 million.

For many professionals in today's Internet-based world, whether advertising is legal, or even controlled, is not the issue. What is more important is their perception that too much of what passes for on- or offline practice growth strategies is just pandering, and it is often more than a little embarrassing.

We get that. As marketing consultants, we hear those concerns from professionals who recognize the need to reach a larger segment of their target populations, but who want to do so in a dignified manner. The question is not **should** you market, but **how** to do so, in a way that properly reflects your status in the community.

In the chapters that follow, we will suggest a variety of ways to do just that. Several of our strategies focus on helping you generate praise from your clients and patients, rather than relying on self-promotion. Receiving five-star reviews, doing expert-interview videos, and enhancing your website with quality content that provides value to your local market are ways to improve both your practice and your value to the community.

This book has been written for practices in all stages of the business cycle. Whether growing, maintaining, or preparing for transfer—every professional practice requires some level of marketing.

For practices that are **referral-based**, an online marketing presence *must* focus on your reputation, since 87 percent of patients who are referred will go first to the Internet for more information about the practice to which they've been directed. (Real Strategic, October 2015).

Have you thought about who might purchase your practice eventually? "Millennials" coming out of school have grown up with the Internet, and they are quite familiar with using it as a marketing tool. Your online footprint will be an important consideration as they value your practice.

In the pages that follow, we'll show you how to think about marketing for whatever phase of your practice you are in, and how to incorporate some of these methods.

To Your Success!

Gordon and Jennine

Chapter One

Finding Bedrock—Know Your Business

When you think about growing your professional practice, what comes to mind? Maybe questions like: where is the best place to buy advertising? Should I open a second office in another part of the city? Are there new practice areas I should consider adding to our services? Is this a good time to add a new associate? I know I need to be online these days, but how do I do that?

These are all *good* questions, but they are the *wrong* questions!

Let us share an experience Gordon had a few years ago after speaking at a marketing seminar. After the presentation, he stayed around to talk with attendees, and hopefully to find a client or two. As he was chatting with several people, a man came up to the group and was obviously anxious to talk. As people drifted away, he blurted out, "I've signed a contract for a full-page ad in the Yellow Pages for the next year, and my ad is due tomorrow. How much will you charge me to write the ad?"

Without a pause, Gordon said, "$5,000."

"What?!" he gasped. "Five grand just to write an ad for the Yellow Pages? That's crazy!"

"Really? Think about it," Gordon replied to the man. "I don't know you. I don't know your company and the products you offer. I don't know your customer, your value proposition, or other advertising you do. If all you want is a list of platitudes and generalities to give the Yellow Pages rep, you certainly don't need me. But if you want the $40,000 you're going to spend over the next year on that full-page ad to actually give you a return on that investment, then I have to know all of those details about your business so I can write an ad that will attract the prospects you want."

He didn't get the job that day, but interestingly enough, that same business owner called us several months later, asked for a meeting, and ultimately hired our company to help them introduce a new product line.

This experience is not unusual. In fact, far too often when we begin a conversation with a prospective client about marketing their practice, they immediately want to talk tactics. "Do you think cable television is a good place to advertise? The local cable company is offering some great programs." Our response to these questions is always the same: "It could be; we'll have to do the research before we can know for sure."

We will say the same thing to you as you begin reading this book on marketing your practice. You were probably attracted by the title, "Total Market Takeover®." It sounds pretty exciting, and while there are numerous marketing tactics that can work, they might not be the best for your company at this time with the marketing budget you have available.

We want you to feel confident that the information you're about to receive is credible, accurate, and most importantly, will make you money. Bookstore shelves are full of books by people who are great at writing books, but short on experience when it comes to real-world results. We challenge you to go to your favorite bookstore and find more than one or two books that actually contain useful advertising advice, with examples that are relevant to you while trying to implement them into your practice. We recognize this is an issue, because we've spent hours at Barnes and Noble, poring over book after book in the sales, advertising, and marketing sections. We have scanned and read through hundreds of websites of so-called advertising experts. Through it all, we've only found a handful of what could be called "authoritative guides" to getting results—that is, making real-world money—through marketing.

We will promise you a few things right now, right up front. First, we promise you that everything you will learn in this book will be applicable to you as the owner, managing partner, or practitioner of your professional practice. We promise you that you won't find yourself wondering, "What in the heck does that have to do with my business?" We promise you that all of the examples shared herein come from real-life, hands-on experiences. We promise you that if you will implement the strategies we share, you will see an immediate impact in the effectiveness of your marketing.

In other words, we promise you that using this information will make you money—and that's the name of the game, right? You didn't pick up a program on marketing for any other reason than to learn how to make more money, did you? Enough of the promises— let's move on to substance!

In this opening chapter, we will share with you the conceptual foundation of Total Market Takeover®. We call this process, "Finding Bedrock." When a contractor begins construction on a high-rise office building, they frequently drill down to "bedrock" and sink the pilings to that level, to give the building a strong foundation. You can think of the concepts we're sharing in this first chapter as the immovable support for your business marketing plans—the "bedrock."

There are four marketing concepts that we believe form the bedrock of the Total Market Takeover® philosophy.

They are:

- The inside reality of your company vs. the outside perception of the marketplace
- Strategic Marketing and Tactical Marketing
- Identifying your Ideal Customer
- Articulating your Value Proposition

We want to begin with these concepts, rather than jump ahead to show you how to design a lead generation website or build an effective pay-per-click campaign. We will cover some tremendously powerful strategies for growing your company, but not until you understand why they can have such an impact.

Inside Reality vs. Outside Perception

There are actually two different sides to your practice. First, there is what we call the "Inside Reality"; secondly, there is the "Outside Perception." The inside reality is all of the things your practice does that make you valuable to your patients and clients...from the services you offer and the products you use, to your business operations and the commitment to excellence of your key team members. It is what gives you a competitive advantage in the marketplace.

The reason we call it the inside *reality* is because there is a good chance that the reality of what you do, and your clients' perceptions of what you do, aren't necessarily the same. You'll find that these two words—reality and perception—are very important to this process of winning the market-share war for your practice.

The inside reality encompasses everything you do and everything you are that makes you good. It is all your skills, your people, your expertise, your service to the client—before, during, *and* after the sale—your systems, your operational procedures, your commitment to exceed client expectations, your passion, and the way you conduct your business. You might think you're actually better than you are—or you might not be giving yourself enough credit for the things you do well. There is a reality of how valuable you are to the marketplace based on these things and others, both tangible and less tangible.

If you ask your clients or patients why they chose to work with you, they could tell you something quantifiable, specific, and instantly obvious. They could point to specific advantages of doing business with you, and say, "That's why I had you _____ (fill in the blank with your service); that's why I refer my friends to you; that's why I'm a fan of the practice."

It's imperative that you begin to innovate your practice so that there's a reason for people to choose you. However, here's the problem: just because you have achieved that level of innovation doesn't mean that patients are going to flock to your office. There's still the job of marketing that has to be done, and that is where the "outside perception" comes into play.

If the inside reality is about what you do and what you are that allows your practice to perform better than your competitors, then the outside perception has to do with how clients and prospects perceive your industry and your company. Invariably, the inside reality and the outside perception are different.

Regardless of how good you are—how excellent your inside reality is—your prospective client is more than likely going to be apathetic. It is not because they don't like you or they think your practice is bad; it is because trying to figure out how good you are is the last thing on their priority list. Ask yourself this question: how many competitors, either direct or indirect, do you have in your practice niches? Whatever that number is, that is how many choices your prospects have, and how many competitors they have to sift through to make a buying decision.

Another challenge is that most professions, at best, command indifference, and at worst, suffer from a negative reputation. Honestly, many of your prospective patients or clients don't know, or care, very much about what you offer. Your product or service meets a need for them, but it doesn't often generate a level of excitement. For many industries and professional niches, the public's general perception trends towards the negative. Think about it—who likes to go see an attorney or dentist, or who gets excited about going to the chiropractor?

As if this general indifference on the part of the public isn't enough of a challenge, the marketing battle for a practice with an excellent inside reality is even more difficult. The problem is that most practices don't have the ability to communicate, via advertising and marketing, their inside reality to the outside world. Even if they are exceptional, they are unable to lead a prospect to the conclusion that it would be absolutely foolish to do business with anyone else but them.

That is the challenge of marketing your practice— conveying the excellent inside reality of your company to a marketplace that tends to look at you and your competitors as basically the same.

The late business speaker Jim Rohn may have summed it up best in his lecture about communication. He was discussing personal, not business, communication, but we think the principles are identical. He asserts that to be a master communicator, all you must do is follow a simple, three-step process. First, have something good to say. Second, say it well. Third, say it often. Does that make sense to you? Have something good to say, say it well, and say it often.

Having something good to say is the inside reality of your business—the excellent people and systems that you have created. The purpose of Total Market Takeover® is to improve the outside perception of your business, or in other words, how to say it well so people will choose you as their product or service provider.

Sometimes when we share these concepts, a business practitioner will say, "Yes, okay, that makes sense to me—the inside reality and the outside perception. But will these marketing strategies you suggest work for ME in MY practice?" The answer is an unqualified "YES!"

We work with owners in a variety of professions, and what we see is that, on the most basic level, all want exactly the same thing—more new clients or patients and less competition. They want to keep their margins, have their marketing and advertising work better, attract and retain more loyal clients, increase the conversion ratios from their advertising...and ultimately, they all want to make more money. True enough?

It is important also to recognize that all prospective clients want the same things. They want the get the best deal, in terms of price and value. They want to feel confident that their money has been spent well and that their decision has been made to the best of their ability. You never hear someone say, "I got bids from four attorneys and negotiated the best deals I could, then finally selected the firm where I got the third-best deal." No! People instinctively want to make the best decision possible.

In this situation, there are two sets of values: the practice wants more patients, with whom they can build loyalty; the patient wants the best possible deal in terms of overall value. The process and principles that govern the matching of these two value sets are exactly the same for every practice.

It is really quite simple: as the business owner, all you must do is demonstrate to your prospective client that you actually *are* the best deal, in terms of price and value; and then, through your marketing campaigns, communicate those reasons to him in a way that he will pay attention to and internalize.

The problem is that a great many practices come nowhere close to holding up their end of the bargain. Most have a tough time distinguishing and differentiating their own practice, and then communicating those advantages in an instantly obvious way. They can't make their outside perception match their inside reality.

Think of it this way. What if you could find a way to propel an additional 20 percent of qualified leads into your practice to what you are finding currently—without increasing your monthly ad spend? Assuming you kept your same closing ratio, what would that extra 20 percent, attained for the same money spent, mean to your bottom line? Then consider this "what if": what if you could draw in 20 percent more qualified prospects, but you could ALSO find a way to increase your conversion ratio by 10 percent—across the board? What would THAT do to your bottom line? We believe that you might be able to achieve those kinds of modest increases just by reading this book and implementing some of the marketing strategies we will teach you.

Now that you understand the terms "inside reality" and "outside perception," and the marketing challenge that is the result, let's conduct a quick attitude check before moving on to the next subject. It doesn't really matter how your practice is doing right now—whether it is growing, declining, or stagnant. Your attitude about winning in business and success is *the most important thing* if you are going to utilize the Total Market Takeover® program successfully. The attitude is: "I'm going to do whatever it takes, as long as it's legal, ethical, and moral, to make my practice as innovative— and therefore valuable—as possible. Because of that, I fully expect to win the lion's share of business...and, quite probably, I will dominate all of my competitors in the process."

That is a bold statement, but you'll realize as you read along that this program is not for business people who just want to get by, or who are looking for the marketing program of the month, or who just want to learn a bunch of tricks and shortcut techniques to success. If that is you, and you're satisfied with hanging out in the middle of the pack, then we recommend you stop reading now because you likely will be frustrated and will have wasted your time.

Let us explain this point in another way. Right after he won his fifth MVP award, Michael Jordan said, "Hey, I'm not sitting around trying to figure out how to be the best player in the league. I'm continually trying to figure out how I can be the best I can be. Then the rest—the MVP awards and championships—will all fall into place."

The people who are successful at implementing the Total Market Takeover® program we're sharing in this book are people who sincerely want to be the best they can be. These are people who have such a passion for their patients and clients, and for doing things right, that they will do whatever it takes to be good enough to deserve all the business. This program is designed for people who can't stomach the thought of a potential client doing business with a competitor. If you strive for that kind of excellence, you will automatically surpass 90 percent of the others in your market niche. They won't put in that kind of effort; they just won't and don't. It is up to you.

That might sound strong, but we hope you feel that about your business. We hope that you would put that kind of effort into perfecting your craft so that it is worthy of the lion's share of the dollars in your industry. If you don't feel that way, and you're not willing to put in that kind of effort, then throw this book away right now and get ready to be clobbered by someone who does feel that way. We guarantee you they are out there. Remember our comment that with the right mindset, you'd pass up 90 percent of your competitors? That also means that 10 percent are left out there trying to dominate the market, and it's going to be a dogfight. To think otherwise would be naïve.

Strategic Marketing and Tactical Marketing

The second foundational principle to understand is the distinction between strategic and tactical marketing. This is important because you want to focus your time where it is most effective. Many practice owners concentrate on tactical marketing; we want to encourage you to give your attention to the strategic side of marketing. Let us begin by defining what those terms mean.

Strategic marketing is what you say, how you say it, and who you say it to. *Tactical marketing* is where you say it. Stated a different way, strategic marketing is your marketing plan—how you define and identify your ideal customer, the target market you are selling to, and the things you are going to say that are specifically relevant to those people. Tactical marketing is how you are going to find them. That might mean advertising on the radio or in the newspaper or changing your website—that's the tactical side.

We know from experience with many business owners that you spend most of your time on the tactical. Here's an example. You decide to run a seasonal promotion, which means you need a display ad into the local newspaper. Immediately, you put together some ideas for the ad, and then call the salesperson at the newspaper to help you with layout. They are more than happy to take your money and put your ad in for the weekend. By the middle of the next week, you are scratching your head and wondering why the phone hasn't been ringing. Has that ever been your experience?

Here's why. We spend our time on tactical marketing (where to say it), when what we really need to be doing is stepping back and focusing on the strategic side (what you say, how you say it, and who you say it to.) One of the people who Gordon learned marketing from years ago had a saying that you might find valuable. The man used to say, "If you want to know what John Smith buys, you have to see the world through John Smith's eyes." As a business owner, you must understand what is important to your customer—the "conversation going on in their mind"— so that you can address their desires.

Regrettably, most of us do not take this approach. We know our service really well, and we know our company and how good we are, so that is the frame of reference we use in our marketing. We write ads that make sense to us and that have a lot of "features," without paying attention to the "benefits" our patients are actually looking for. This is why there are so many ads in the marketplace with ludicrous platitudes, declaring things like, "we are the best," "in business for 39 years," "we do quality work," and "our staff is friendly." Are statements like these of any value to a prospective client who is deciding whether to do business with your practice or with a competitor?

As a practice owner, how *do* you know how John Smith sees the world? How *do* you know what John Smith's eyes are looking for? The answer is simple—you ask John. That is what you must do—get inside the minds of your patients and potential patients. You've got to figure out what they like and what they don't like. This might sound elementary, but we're telling you flat-out that almost nobody does it!

In his book, "7 Habits of Highly Effective People," author Stephen Covey discusses this concept. He writes, "Seek first to understand, then to be understood." In reality, most practices seek first to be understood. They will open the doors for business, build a website, run ads, or hire an ad agency—all to run around in the marketplace saying the same thing: "Here we are. Come buy from us."

Whenever they create new strategies, ads, or marketing pieces, they try to figure out what new gimmicks, tricks, and techniques they can use to attract more patients. Practice owners are repeatedly asking, "What can we do or say that will get clients in the door?" Instead, the more appropriate question they should ask is, "What do patients want or need to hear, and in what format and medium will they accept the message?"

Identifying Your Ideal Client

This may seem obvious—you may be saying to yourself, "My ideal client is someone who needs (fill in the blank with the service you offer). This is true, but by generalizing your client to be just anyone who needs what you offer, you force yourself into spending your marketing budget merely advertising for leads. That means you are using multi-media like radio, television, direct mail, and other print options; working with "leads" companies; joining networking groups and associations; hiring outside salespeople; paying for website and search-engine optimization services; and other generic lead-generation activities. We know that this is what most practices do to create new business, but what if there were a more effective way? One that was not only more effective, but a marketing plan that allowed you to calculate the actual return on investment for your monthly spend?

Fortunately, there is. This book will help you focus on specific strategies to maximize the impact of your advertising dollars. To begin, we will explain the difference between a defined and a non-defined market, and then give you a technique for accurately identifying your ideal client.

A *defined marketplace* is one in which you can identify, pinpoint, and obtain a list of people who are prospective clients for your practice. A *non-defined market* is just the opposite—you have to advertise to create leads to begin the marketing process.

The more you can define your marketplace, the more effective your marketing is going to be; the more profitable your practice will be. We once heard Dan Kennedy say, "If everybody is your customer, then nobody is your customer." It truly makes sense. If you are trying to sell to anyone and everyone in your city, you have a tough challenge. To the extent that you can narrow the market down and identify specific people or groups who are potential prospects, it makes your marketing that much more effective.

How is this done? Here are several ideas:

1. <u>What services do you offer</u>? It is not sufficient to think in generalities—not just, "I'm a chiropractor," or "We're a business law firm." Be very specific about each product or service you have available. Focus on the details: "I'm a chiropractor who specializes in chiropractic orthopedics, and I also work with infants and children up to age ten." Or, "Our law firm helps new and growing businesses establish the correct entity structure and internal documentation to ensure a proper legal foundation."

Begin the ideal customer identification process by first segmenting your products and services, almost like each was a separate business. Each service has one or more ideal customers you can specifically identify, and then market to.

2. <u>Think about the demographics in your market area</u>. From which part(s) of town are you currently getting most of your business? Is that where you really want to

be? Are there neighborhoods or surrounding communities that you would like to have more business in? Is your professional office limited to potential patients or clients within a geographic radius (or do you believe you are)?

3. <u>Where do your ideal prospects gather in the greatest numbers</u>? What other businesses or organizations transact business with them? How can you obtain or build a list using their other interests and involvements?

4. <u>How do your ideal clients like to be communicated with</u>? What do they read? Who do they listen to? Are they active on social media, or do they still consult the Yellow Pages? Do they carry smart phones?

An easy way to begin to identify your ideal client is to look at clients you have served in the past year. Here are some questions to ask about them:

- Who made the decision to work with you? What is their gender, age, income, and occupation?
- Where, exactly, did they live? (Get a map of your area, and use pushpins to mark every client's address.)
- How did they hear about you? How did they contact you, or did you make the initial contact with them?

- Why did they choose you rather than a competitor? Be honest with yourself here. If you are willing to discount your fees to get the deal, then recognize that fact.
- What, if any, continuing contact have you had with the client since their last visit or purchase?

Now, what do you do with this data? Initially, you should be able to quantify some information about your practice and the success of your marketing efforts as a result of doing this analysis.

As you look at the patient profile that emerges, ask yourself if this is the "who" you want to continue to market to. If so, then you'll be pleased with the strategies we will share with you in the coming chapters. They will help you target your ideal patients more accurately and at a lower cost than much of what you are doing today.

If not—if you want to grow your practice with a different client profile—then we will show you how to do that. For example, we worked with a chiropractor who had a modest-sized practice, in a middle-class neighborhood on the west side of his city. He asked if we could help him gain exposure in the suburbs on the south side, a more affluent area where he thought there might be greater interest in his services. After analyzing the market, we designed campaigns using real-time bidding, focusing on the neighborhoods he had targeted. We placed his ad in front of homeowners in those neighborhoods as they went online. The cost was very reasonable—less than $5.00 for one thousand impressions! Within a few weeks, he began to get calls from the south side. The added revenue from the first few patients paid for his entire yearly marketing budget!

There is a chapter devoted to real-time bidding later in the book.

Articulating Your Value Proposition

The final piece to your well-constructed marketing foundation is to define your value proposition. That is, "Why should a prospective client choose your practice instead of your competitors?" One of the reasons we suggested that you spend time identifying your ideal prospect(s) is because it is likely you have a different value proposition for each one. The value proposition should answer the questions: "Why should I buy *this* product or service?" as well as, "Why should I do anything at all?" It is a clear and specific statement about the tangible benefits of your offer, and it should be stated in terms understood and accepted by the target patient.

First, we'll suggest a way to think through and write out your value proposition, then give some examples for different clients. The first portion of the value proposition asserts the value of the offering in terms of the results and benefits; it demonstrates how you are equipped to deliver that value (it notes your skills and abilities).The second sentence asserts the positioning of that value by establishing a contrast.

First Sentence:

- Because we have *(skills, experience, knowledge or other attribute),*
- We are able to *(provide service, fix the problem, or other deliverable);*
- This means *(benefits the client will value),*
- For *(the client).*

Second (optional) Sentence:

- Unlike *(primary competitive alternative),*
- Our service *(statement of primary differentiation).*

Following are some examples of how a CPA firm might articulate a different value proposition for three categories of clients they serve:

First, marketing to a small business owner:

"Because we have specialists who focus on the unique challenges of the small business owner, we are able to offer you a tax professional who can advise you throughout the year on ways to minimize your tax obligation. This means that you can focus on building your business, confident that at the end of the year you will retain as much revenue as possible."

Second, marketing to a professional practice owner who wants to retire in ten years:

"Because we have specialists who understand the unique succession and transition challenges of the professional practice owner, we are able to offer you a team of business planning and tax professionals who can advise you on the medium- and long-term strategies to maximize your practice asset. This means that when the time is right for you to retire, you will be able to market your practice at an optimum price in the marketplace."

Third, marketing a general tax practice to homeowners:

"As a local firm here in (your town), we have earned a reputation for thorough and accurate tax returns over the last (number of years in business). We are full-time tax professionals, not "grocery store" accountants who help you fill out a standardized form. This enables us to offer homeowners the most thorough tax analysis and return preparation, taking advantage of all the deductions you are legally entitled to. Additionally, we will help you create a strategy for this year, to minimize your tax obligations next spring."

We hope you are beginning to see the importance of a clear value proposition, tailored to each type of client you work with. As you can see in these examples for a CPA firm, the value proposition is essentially the same for each of these target prospects, but the application is personalized to their individual interests.

Your value proposition cannot be a series of platitudes and generalities. It must draw a line in the sand between you and your competitors, clearly stating the benefit to the client of working with your firm.

WHAT TO DO NOW:

1. Take a long, hard look at your inside reality. Are your people, systems, and physical location the best they can be? Is everyone on your team trained not only for their specific job, but do they also understand the "mission-vision-values" of your practice? The bottom line question is this: are you deserving of the majority of business in your market?

If not, what needs to be innovated in your practice to

put yourself in a position to become the dominant provider?

This can be a difficult, and maybe even painful, process. Every one of us wants to believe that we offer an excellent value to our clients and patients; yet, it is easy to get so involved in the daily operation of our practice that we don't step back to take a realistic appraisal of how a prospect might see us.

One of Gordon's previous businesses was a mortgage company. Twice a year, the management team held a two-day meeting, away from the office. They focused the first day on looking at every customer comment card and each step in every process within the company. They started with how the phone was answered, looking at every stage, up to the communication had with a borrower after their loan had closed.

The second day was spent innovating those systems to make them more customer-centric. It was hard work— two very long days! However, each "retreat" resulted in a better inside reality.

You may not need a two-day marathon like his company did, but involving several people from your team, as well as clients, in the evaluation of your practice will help you quickly gauge what you can do to create an excellent inside reality.

2. Determine whether you have a strategic marketing plan. Is it written, with timelines and a budget for implementation of each tactic you want to employ...or are you reacting every time a shiny new marketing idea comes across your desk?

Without a clearly defined marketing strategy, you are wasting money! Invest the time necessary to identify who your ideal prospect is, two or three methods of communicating with them, and allocate a budget that will enable you to fund the proper marketing tactics.

3. Identify at least three unique client groups to whom you would like to market your company. This can be geographical, but challenge yourself to go deeper than just focusing on a part of your city. Think about both demographic and psychographic characteristics.

When we work with a client, we call this process "developing your client avatars." The result of the process for them is a highly detailed profile of each ideal patient or client, which includes their "name," type of work they do, income range, where they live, family size, car they drive, where they shop, what kind of vacations they take, movies they like, and more.

The reason this is such an important exercise is that when you begin to design your marketing plan, knowing specifically who you are marketing to will help you determine *what* to say and *how* to say it (strategic marketing). Once you have your marketing messages clear, your patient avatar will dictate *where* you say it (tactical marketing).

4. Develop a value proposition for each of your ideal clients. Concentrate on the benefits to the client and what makes you different from the other service providers who might make them an offer.

It is your value propositions that form the basis of the advertising that you will write. Whether it is a radio spot, pay-per-click ad, or direct-mail piece, it must focus on the value you bring to the prospect.

As you can see, these are interrelated activities. As a general rule you'll start with looking at your inside reality, but as you drill down on who your ideal client is, you may realize you need to innovate in a way you had not anticipated. Delivering on the value proposition(s) you want to offer might require equipment or personnel that you don't have at this time.

CONCLUSION

Recall that this chapter is titled, "Finding Bedrock." These preliminary activities are the foundation of an effective and profitable marketing strategy for your practice. They are synergistic. Before spending money on a specific business growth strategy, we encourage you to invest time defining these foundational concepts.

Chapter Two

Reputation Marketing—Your Business is "In The Stars"

We are not exaggerating when we say that, in the last eighteen months, controlling and marketing your reputation online has become the single-most critical aspect of any online marketing you can do for your practice. This task is completely different from the search-engine optimization (SEO) or social media marketing that is the mainstream, and which you probably have companies calling every week and offering to do for you. The reality is that the strategy for online marketing of your professional practice forever changed in September of 2014. Did you know that?

In August 2014, the search engines dramatically changed their algorithms for ranking websites. This was not only Google—Bing and Yahoo rewrote their programs at the same time. The major change is that, prior to that time, the position where your site appeared on the search-engine results page was the product of a complicated calculation that included several variables; it was most heavily weighted by the number of "backlinks" connected to your site. It was a relatively simple matter for those in the SEO business to artificially manufacture these backlinks. That meant that we could take a website and drive it to the first pages of the search engines, strictly using technology, without regard to how many people might actually be looking for or finding value on the website.

The important change that was implemented replaced backlinks with a practice's reputation as a primary criteria for page rank; this reputation is defined by actual patients who have used your service and then posted a review of their experience online. The search engines now send their spiders through several hundred "review sites," looking for comments about your practice. When they find one, it is harvested and combined with other reviews in a formula that results in a "Star Rating" for your business. One star is bad; five stars is the best.

This is a game-changer for how to market your practice online. In this chapter, we will share with you how our firm has reacted to this new paradigm for our clients, and what you can do to ride effectively and profit from the reputation wave. The reality is that most professional practice managers are far too busy to try to keep track of changes that the search engines make. When a major change like this occurs, it can take a long time for the business community to react. That is good news for you reading this chapter—you can be the market leader in your area. In detail, we will cover:

- Specific game changers and how they impact your business
- What your prospects are looking for today in choosing a business to work with
- What is "Reputation Marketing"
- How to get a free report showing your company's online reputation
- A four-step strategy to make your company the reputation market leader
- Questions about reputation marketing that we often hear

Obviously, you are aware that every day, people go online searching for a product or service vendor. Do you know just how many people are searching? The answer might surprise you. At the time of this writing, February 2016, we asked one of our support team members to do a quick analysis of how many people searched for a family dentist in several cities around the country. Following is the number of people who search *each month*, on average, in each of these cities:

Phoenix, AZ	2,845
Miami, FL	3,360
Charlotte, NC	1,410

Portland, OR	1,655
Des Moines, IA	820
Columbus, OH	2,775
Pittsburgh, PA	1,980

Can you imagine hundreds, if not thousands, of people online every single month, looking for your services. The real question is, can they find you? Every day, people in your community are looking for a (your business.) As they do so, they are asking themselves these questions: "Who should I choose? Who can I trust?" What they're doing is looking for the most reputable company. Applying the concepts in this chapter can ensure that you are the business they call, and not your competitor.

Here is another question. Think about your own process when you are looking for a specific product or service. Would you buy from a company that has bad ratings and reviews? Most likely, you obviously wouldn't. A more realistic way to think about that question follows.

Three companies are, for all practical purposes, identical. All three have what you are looking for, and the price point is the same. One company has six good reviews, the other has four good and one bad review; the third has no reviews at all. Which one do you buy from? Almost everyone would choose the company with six good reviews. Why is that? Of course, we want to have a great buying experience too. We are looking to see that a company is consistent in delivering that experience or that product or service that we want to buy.

This is exactly what prospects looking for what you offer do every single day. They go online and search to find the most reputable practice to work with. Only one bad review can send the prospect from your website or your listing online to someone else. That means the difference between your phone ringing or your competition's phone ringing.

Game-Changers That Affect Your Practice Today

Game-Changer Number One. When you do a search for any practice specialty and its city, the resulting list reveals the practice's reputation. Following is a random example of a search for a criminal attorney in Columbus, OH.

Luftman, Heck & Associates, LLP
4.9 ★★★★★ (49) · Criminal Justice Attorney
580 E Rich St · (614) 500-3836
Open 24 hours

Website   Directions

Joslyn Law Firm
4.8 ★★★★★ (20) · Criminal Justice Attorney
501 S High St · (614) 444-1900
Open until 10:00 PM

Website   Directions

The Koffel Law Firm
4.7 ★★★★⯨ (16) · Criminal Justice Attorney
1801 Watermark Dr #350 · (614) 675-4845
Open 24 hours

Website   Directions

After entering the search term, we were taken to a page that featured these firms in the "three-pack." As you can see, all three of these firms have a high reputation score or star rating. Also notice that each firm has quite a few reviews; sixteen is the fewest. It is not coincidence that these practices are listed in this highly coveted space on the first page of the search results; they all have excellent ratings.

Here is why this game-changer is so important: anyone searching for a professional practice listing, even just for directions or to get the phone number, is going to see the practice's reputation as well. This is done automatically by the search engines; as a business, you have no control over your reputation being shown. Consider the situation where someone recommends your firm to a friend. According to international marketing firm Real Strategic, there is an 87 percent probability that the person will look up your company online…maybe just to get the phone number. If you have a poor review score, what are the chances they are going to call you? Even though they were referred, which in the past was almost a guarantee that you would get an opportunity to bid for that business, if your reputation score is less than four stars, they will probably go elsewhere.

Ask yourself this: when someone types in your practice name, what will they find? What is your reputation score? Does it show no reviews at all, or some good and others not-so-good? Go to Google and see.

Game-Changer Number Two. Customer reviews are now a major factor in almost every type of online marketing, and it is all done automatically. Your reviews, good and bad, show up in Google maps and your Google-plus listing (and the same for the other search engines, too). Your star rating is included in your pay-per-click ads. The reviews show up on organic website listings. They show up in local directories like Yelp and City Search and Bing and Yahoo, and also in the online Yellow Pages. Reviews are now a major factor in almost every type of online marketing. Like it or not, everyone searching for your practice or in your category will see them.

<u>Game-Changer Number Three</u>. All of this points to the reality that SEO, social media, PPC, local marketing—all of the strategies we have refined online for the past five or more years—none of them are effective anymore if you have bad reviews or a bad reputation online.

Think carefully about this next concept—especially those of you who have done it yourself or paid someone to do online marketing for you...or maybe you're still paying. Why would you want to do all that work, spend all the time and money getting to the top of the search engines, and then when people find you, they see bad reviews? You have just wasted your resources!

In our firm over the last year, we have done a complete flip-flop in our online marketing strategy. Previously, we would start with Google maps, then we would do Yelp and video marketing. We did blogging, social media, and press releases, and our tech people would create link wheels, all designed to help our clients get to the first page for their primary keywords. Now, that is completely the opposite of what today's marketing is about.

The very first step if you want to be effective in marketing online today is creating a five-star reputation. *Then, and only then,* you market your services online, because your phone is not going to ring if you don't have that five-star reputation your prospects are looking for.

What Prospective Clients Are Seeking Today

There are definitely some down-sides to the impact that "reputation" has made, but there are some very positive game-changers that are a result of this emphasis on reputation, as well.

<u>Game-Changer Number Four</u>. Reviews send you prequalified, presold clients; the reason is because buyers trust reviews as much as personal recommendations. Reviews can be incredibly bad for you if they're bad, but they can be incredibly good for you if they are truly good. Myles Anderson at BrightLocal has noted that 72 percent of buyers trust reviews as much as they trust personal recommendations.

72% Of Buyers Trust Reviews As Much As Personal Recommendations

About The Author: Myles Anderson is Founder & CEO of BrightLocal.com. BrightLocal

Stop to think about growing your practice. Would you rather create a marketing plan that focuses on people who don't know you, don't necessarily like you, don't trust you, and always are worried about price...or would you rather create a marketing plan that attracts people who feel they know you, who already like and trust you, and who act like they are all referrals?

Of course you want the latter—you want to create a referral-based marketing plan. For the first time ever, our online marketing can be just as powerful as referral marketing. This is because three out of four people trust reviews just as much as personal recommendations!

We need those five-star reviews on your website and on your listings. That is as good as someone's mother recommending that you get your service from this firm, or someone's best friend saying, "You know what? You should call ABC and Associates; I used them and they were amazing." Having positive reviews is just as good as a colleague at work saying, "Look, if you need a new (your service), you should go to this office. They do a great job!" You can think of it that way, because 72 percent of buyers trust reviews just as much as personal recommendations.

Reviews are powerful marketing that you need for your business. Here is more proof.

You likely are familiar with the Nielsen ratings; for years, they have been one of the top-rated data collection companies in the world. When inquiring to find the extent to which people trust different forms of advertising, Nielsen found some startling facts.

To what extent do you trust the following forms of advertising?

Global Average	Trust Completely/ Somewhat	Don't Trust Much/ At All
Recommendations from people I know	92%	8%
Consumer opinions posted online	70%	30%
Editorial content such as newspaper articles	58%	42%
Branded Websites	58%	42%
Emails I signed up for	50%	50%
Ads on TV	47%	53%
Text ads on mobile phones	29%	71%

Source: Nielsen Global Trust in Advertising Survey, Q3 2011

Ninety-two percent of people trust recommendations from people that they know. That is not too surprising, but look at what came in second. Seventy percent of people trust opinions in online reviews. This corroborates the report from BrightLocal, which declared that 72 percent trust reviews. Essentially that is three out of every four people!

A little further down the page, the results show that survey respondents actually trust consumer opinions expressed in reviews from complete strangers posted online more than an editorial or newspaper article. You could actually have a newspaper article written about you, and people will not trust that as much as an online review. As you can see, the evidence points to the fact that reputation marketing is the most important marketing that you can do. If you are going to do any type of marketing for your practice, it should not start with the type of marketing that people don't trust, like television ads at 47 percent or email marketing at 50 percent, or even branded website marketing at 58 percent. Your marketing should start with the top two: recommendations from people that people know, and consumer opinions posted online—this is "reputation marketing."

If you are not yet convinced why having a five-star reputation is so vital to practice growth, here is one more statistic. Consumers look up an average of ten reviews before making a decision. What does this mean for you? First, all of these consumers are online, and they are looking for reviews. Second, and more importantly, they are looking at multiple reviews, not just one or two.

For those of you who have been wondering to yourselves how many reviews is enough, here is your answer. Seventy percent of consumers trust a practice with a minimum of six to ten reviews, meaning that, at the least, you need to have six, five-star reviews. Another fact—the search engines place a greater emphasis on reviews that are less than six months old. Having eight reviews, three of which are over a year old, actually hurts your placement in the search results.

The reality of the marketplace today is that you are not credible without five-star reviews. Without a five-star reputation and a minimum of six to ten reviews, your practice won't be trusted when people actually find you. This is the difference between your phone ringing and it not ringing. More importantly, this is the difference between your phone not ringing and your competitor's phone ringing.

So What Exactly is Reputation Marketing?

Reputation marketing is building a five-star reputation online, and then going out and marketing that reputation. It is positioning your company in front of thousands of buyers, as the market leader with a five-star reputation. As discussed previously, this is the most powerful and trusted type of marketing you can do to grow your professional practice in today's market.

The bottom line is, how do you create a reputation marketing program? Following is the step-by-step strategy.

What is Your Online Reputation Today?

The first step is to understand, truly, your current reputation. Do you know your online reputation? Do you know what people are saying about you right now? If you don't, there is a way to gather the information quickly and at no cost. Alchemy Consulting has created a proprietary system and software that actually reveals to any practice, within just a few minutes, what their online reputation is; this system uses the practice phone number to acquire the data. Following, we describe the report that you will receive, then we give you the link to get one for your practice.

When you enter your *primary business telephone* number, the software will search more than three dozen review websites, locations like Yelp, the Yellow Pages, Citysearch, and others. In about one minute, a report will be created that shows you two primary pieces of data.

First, it includes the number of bad reviews that exist on the World Wide Web about your practice. A Reputation Score will be calculated, based on the ratio between good and bad reviews that are found. At the bottom of the report will be a copy of every negative listing, including what the person said and the location where we found it. Secondly, we will also check the primary review sites to see if your company listing on those sites has been claimed. "Claiming" your listing is important because that allows you to respond when someone posts a negative review about your company; these sites are crawled by the search-engine spiders, so having claimed the site and ensured the information is accurate is important.

You can generate your *free* reputation report at this URL:

www.ReputationMaverick.com

The report will serve as a baseline for your reputation marketing program. Getting this free report is where you begin, then, once you know your reputation, you will be able to see which of the four reputation types you have currently. These definitions follow:

The first is a bad reputation. Obviously, that is not what you are striving for and you will want to do something about it—fast. Second is no reputation at all, which is no more valuable than having a bad reputation—no reviews won't get your phone ringing. Remember, you need at least six to ten, five-star reviews to look credible online. Third is a good reputation. If you have a good reputation, that simply means you have some good reviews, and maybe some not-so-good reviews...but more good than bad.

Lastly, what if you have ten really good reviews, but the last two are bad? This is the question we looked at earlier; if you had multiple good reviews but one bad review versus another practice who was positive on all reviews, who would you go with? Having a good reputation score is not enough. It is getting a five-star reputation that is going to make you the industry leader.

How is that done? Here are the steps that we follow, and you may "swipe and deploy" them for your practice.

A Four-Step Strategy to Make Your Company the Reputation Market Leader

This image is an overview of the four-step process for creating a five-star online reputation.

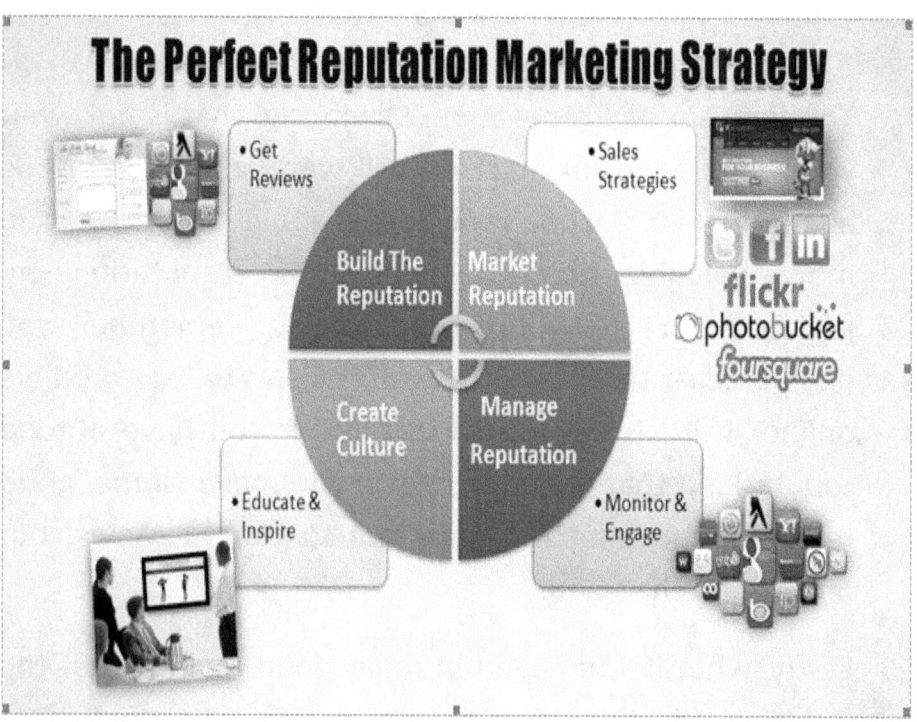

Step one is building your reputation; you want to develop the five-star reputation that is the foundation of all your marketing online. The second step is to market that reputation so that prospects looking for the services you offer will choose you.

The third step is ongoing management of your reputation. This is not one of those "one and done" processes; you want to continue to keep your five-star reputation going. In reality, you are only one customer away from a bad review. Think about it—everyone has a bad day on occasion: the receptionist, hygienist or other team member, or even you. Every one of our businesses is just one day and one client away from a bad review. So we want to keep our "eyes on the ball," to make sure we stay focused.

The last component of a perfect reputation marketing strategy is to create a reputation marketing culture in your office. It is not enough to attempt to fix things after the fact. We want your practice to be proactive inside, to make sure that every single person in your practice is on the same page. We want your entire team motivated to do one thing: a great job for your patients, giving them a first-class experience and receiving a five-star review to keep that five-star reputation going.

We will focus more deeply on the first component: developing your five-star reputation.

There are a variety of ways to do this. One of the best

strategies, and easiest to implement quickly, is to create professionally designed review postcards. We design these for our clients, and then they have them printed and sent to their clients. These are quite powerful, and they invite the client to give a five-star review. Another technique we use is to design and print a business-card invitation to leave a five-star review. This is important, because your staff needs to be armed with a way to help patients give you reviews. Giving patients a business card that tells them where they can place the review, and how easily it can be done, is vital for creating a five-star reputation. Following is an example of the business card tool.

Another tool we provide is templates for email. Emails are very easy ways to get reviews, but you have to word the copy in such a way that your patients are motivated to not only to read, but to take action. We provide these templates for our clients. Certainly, there are other techniques for inviting clients to give you a five-star review, but these are three that you can apply your business today.

One of the most powerful insider strategies that we create for our clients is a private review page. This is actually a webpage; it has its own distinct URL. Our goal is a one-stop shop for everyone to be able to post their reviews.

The thinking behind this technique is, would you rather someone post a review on Yelp that's not–so-good, or would you prefer they put it on your own personal review page where you can see it before it is published? That is the power of the private review page; all customer reviews are funneled into one place. As they come in, only the four- and five-star reviews are allowed to be forwarded onto the internet review sites. For those reviews that are less favorable, three stars or less, we send our client a private email to alert them. This is so that they can speak with their dissatisfied client to resolve any issues, before their client posts a review online that doesn't reflect a five-star reputation.

Another point—having a posting strategy is critical, and here is the reason. Many of our clients have collected reviews and testimonials from their patients in the past. Often, they create a testimonial page on their website and post the reviews on that page. You may have some of these, too.

However, if you were to post these reviews for yourself on several of the review sites, you would find they are deleted within a day or two. The reason is that every one of the different review sites has created an algorithm that recognizes the source of a review, and it filters and deletes all reviews that are posted from the same computer IP network. Even if you have your staff post reviews, they will not be held on the review site. To counteract this reality, we have developed a proprietary system that can post reviews for a company without being filtered or defeated.

Going into more detail on the second quadrant of the perfect reputation marketing strategy, once you actually build a five-star reputation, how do you market it to attract more clients? Using a variety of approaches gives the best results.

If you think that text reviews or reviews posted to a website are powerful, video reviews are that much more potent. Video is especially "hot" right now, and a video review converts like crazy. You do *not* need a lot of expensive cameras or fancy processing software. In another chapter in this book, we will discuss the power of video and give you some easy ways to implement a video marketing program.

Another way to market your five-star reputation is on your website. Do you have reviews on the front page of your website right now—on the home page? Not on a testimonial page buried somewhere on your site, but right there on the home page? Often, that is the most effective location; many times that is the only page a prospect will visit. If your website is built on a WordPress platform, you can add a widget that will post the latest reviews to the sidebar on the home page, scrolling in real time. Talk with the person that built your site and see if you can add this.

Think about how powerful it would be to have a prospective client visiting your site, trying to decide if they should call your practice, when suddenly a new five-star review pops up. That is in addition to the excellent reviews that are already there on the homepage.

This is an important point to remember. You want to continually be updating your reviews so that the most current are easily found. Your prospects are looking for the most recent feedback from your clients—six- or nine-month-old reviews just won't do it.

You will also want to post your five-star reviews on the social media sites to which you belong. With all of the talk about social media in the last couple of years, for many practices it has been a disappointment as far as generating new patients. That changes when you use reputation marketing in your social media. When five-star reviews are being posted several times each week, your Facebook page becomes an incredibly powerful source of leads.

In light of the Nielsen stats we reviewed previously, it would be easy to overlook email marketing. While email marketing by itself may have lost some of its effectiveness, incorporating a five-star reputation into email marketing creates a real synergy. Every time you send an offer, every time you provide a discount, whenever you send out newsletters or any type of email marketing, include at least one, five-star review. Whatever landing page or offer site you direct people to, make sure it has reviews for them to read. This combination will be incredibly powerful for you.

Maps, or "places," marketing is another significant strategy. Have you optimized your maps listing? Other than PPC, this is the best way to have your company listing appear on the first page of the search engines. On Google, we call it the three-pack, because they allow up to three businesses to be listed.

Phase Three of the Perfect Reputation Marketing Strategy is to manage your five-star reputation. The truth of it is that the only effective method is to monitor each and every review site, each day. This is different than monitoring your brand using a tool like Google Alerts. Google Alerts, as well as other similar products, will search the entire web for your business name, your product name, or the name of your CEO. This does not help when someone posts a review, since they are typically doing it on your listing at one of the review sites, and they likely never mention your name at all. You can have all the alerts you want from these monitoring tools, but none of them are programmed to show your reviews.

The reason it is so important to know, rapidly, what reviewers are saying about you online is so you can promptly respond. Many times, a patient will "vent" about their experience using one of the review sites. If you can react within a short period of time, and respond to their concern in a reasonable way and make a genuine offer to resolve their issue, it will enhance your character in the online community. In most cases, the patient will be appeased, and others who come to the site and read the string of comments/responses will recognize you as a responsible professional who cares about resolving patient issues.

Obviously, there are times when a patient is just unreasonable, or flat-out wrong in what they say and expect. You engage them in conversation and attempt to calm the situation, but even if you are not successful with that patient, your responses will demonstrate to prospective clients your willingness to be reasonable.

The bottom line is that you *must* respond! Ignoring negative reviews is the worst policy.

It is not just the negatives though; when you get a positive review, you want to know about that, don't you? Here again, you want to respond and thank the patient. This is also an ideal time to ask them for referrals to someone they know who might need your services.

As you may or may not be aware, several review sites actually aggregate reviews. So when a bad review is posted in one place, it will show up on other websites and other directories. You definitely don't want that happening. This, again, is why a personal review page for your clients is vital for filtering out any bad reviews that you might be getting, before they actually hit the web.

Step Four of the perfect reputation marketing program is to create awareness in the mind of everyone in your practice about the importance of giving five-star service to all clients and prospects. We call this "Building a Reputation Marketing Culture," and there are several things you can do to make it happen for your company.

We use video—specifically a series of five, short (ten minutes or fewer) videos that are focused on the importance of the practice's reputation. We put together a Training Center with some short quizzes for employees, so our clients can be sure their people are learning the concepts. Additionally, if you like video as a training method, there are numerous, customer-focused training videos on YouTube that you can use.

If you have monthly staff meetings with all of your employees, this is an excellent time to discuss client-service techniques. Sharing reviews that have come from clients with your entire team helps them to understand how important each interaction can be. Another technique is occasionally to bring in a customer-service training specialist to work with your people. You should be able to find a local consultant who specializes in this area.

Some Questions About Reputation Marketing

A question that comes up a lot is, "I had someone leave a bad review on Yelp; how can I delete it?"

The short answer is that you can't. We know that there are companies out there who promise to eliminate past bad reviews, but the truth is, it's just not possible. The only real solution is to focus on generating as many four- and five-star reviews as you can, as quickly as possible. Most of the sites display reviews in the order of most-recent first. Over a few months, you will be able to "push down" the bad review so not as many people see it.

There is also an "aging" component to the calculation used to determine your star rating. The most recent reviews are given a greater emphasis by the review sites that aggregate reviews and apply a rating number.

The only exception to this is your Facebook business page. If someone says something negative there, you or your page administrator can delete the conversation. The challenge is that you have to monitor Facebook frequently so that you can stop a problem before it goes viral.

Another question we frequently hear is from practice owners with multiple locations is, "How do the search engines determine the reputation of our firm if we're in several towns?" If you have multiple offices, the reality is that while it is the same company, it is seen as individual locations to the search engines and to the prospective clients looking for what you offer in each city. That means you need to do all of the work of claiming your listing on the review sites and building your "places" page—for each of the search engines, for every location. If you have offices in three cities, you will need three places pages and you will need to claim the top dozen or sites, at a minimum, for each location.

What if you operate multiple businesses from the same location? Keep in mind that most of the review sites use your primary business telephone number as their method of identifying your company. If you do manage several businesses using the same main number, you'll need to distinguish between each of them in the description section of the listings you claim.

We believe that the topic of reputation marketing is so important that we have conducted several web presentations on the subject. One of these was created specifically for the roofing industry, and it is available to watch if you'd like more detail about how to create a program for your practice. While contractors are particularly addressed in the presentation, the principles are the same for your practice. You can watch the replay at: http://0s4.com/r/I8DMWS. This is a recording of a live presentation, so questions from people attending the web presentation are answered—some of the same questions we have addressed in this chapter. There are also some "on the screen" items referenced that you won't see when watching the replay.

Whether you follow some of the steps we have outlined in this chapter and on the webinar, or use another system for getting and marketing positive reviews for your company, reputation marketing is vital to your ability to gain market share and increase profitability. Start today!

WHAT TO DO NOW:

1.   If you haven't already done so, go to www.ReputationMaverick.com and get your free Reputation Report. This will show you the patient comments currently online.

2. The report shows a compilation of the top-listing sites (based on the amount of traffic they get each month). A professional practice should be listed on, at minimum, the following sites: Google+, Yelp, Foursquare, Insider Pages, Citysearch, and Superpages. Keep in mind that most of these sites have an option to pay monthly for an "upgraded" listing. This is not necessary; you can just use the free services.

Finding and claiming your business on these sites can be a little confusing. You can Google the instructions for each one—for example, "How do I register my business on Foursquare?" Then just follow the directions.

3. You also want to claim your "places" listing on Google, Bing, and Yahoo. These require more information to be fully optimized, and the exact steps are frequently updated. Again, a Google search can be made on how to claim and complete your listings.

4. Decide how you are going to invite past patients to review. At the very least, you will want to contact all

patients from the past year. A postcard with instructions and a link to where you'd like them to leave their review works well. Realize that you'll have to send these cards four or five times over a couple of months to get a good response. A phone call at about the time the postcard arrives will increase response rates.

5. Where will you have your clients post their reviews? Obviously, the best option is to have your webmaster create a page like we use, which allows you to exercise more control over the reviews that actually are posted to the web. If that is not feasible, then we suggest you identify the top twenty-five clients who you believe will give you a five-star review, and contact them by phone. Be ready to give them the link to where you'd like the review posted. If they are willing to give you a five-star review, the easiest way to accomplish this is to ask for their email, then send them a thank-you with the link to two of the sites where you would like them to post their review. Google+ and Yelp are the two most-readily recognized sites. You won't go wrong encouraging your clients to post reviews there.

6. Every time you have a meeting with your employees, include a conversation about patient service and the importance of creating a five-star reputation online. Read the reviews that have been posted to your team. Anytime someone on your team is mentioned in a

positive comment from a patient, make sure that is posted for all to see. Some of our clients even offer a small cash bonus ($20 or so) to a team member who is singled out for providing excellent service. The point is to make everyone aware of the role they play in this important focus.

CONCLUSION

We began this chapter with a bold statement: "Controlling and marketing your reputation online has become the single-most critical aspect of any online marketing you do for your practice."

Hopefully, we have helped you realize the truth of this statement, and you are eager begin (or continue) the process of building and marketing your five-star reputation today.

Chapter Three

Lead Generation Website—
A Way to "Start the Conversation" with
Prospective Clients

Would it surprise you to learn that half of the small business owners in America today do not see the value in having a website for their business? That is according to *Entrepreneur* magazine, who researched the question in a national survey. In a similar study Yodle, the online marketing firm, calculated 52 percent of businesses do not have a website.

This begs the obvious question: do you? If the answer is yes, is your website bringing new prospects to your business? Do you know? How can you turn your website into a "leads machine"?

This chapter will cover websites, but it will particularly focus on one specific type of site—the "Lead Generation" website. Here is what we are going to share:

- The four types of websites
- An example of a "Lead Gen" website
- The Educational Spectrum

- The Marketing Equation
- The method to create your own lead gen website

In broad terms, there are four types of websites. Following is a brief description, and how each might apply to a professional practice.

First is the "Business Card" (or "Brochure" or "Static") website; this is the most common type of site. The frequent phone calls and email offers you might be getting, offering to build a website for your company— this is the style of site they have in mind.

In fact, this type of site is so pervasive that there are several "auto builders" you can use to build your own website in a couple of hours. For example, if you buy your web address through GoDaddy, they will immediately offer you their "website tonight" builder program, enabling you to have a multi-page site loaded and working in an evening. These sites are quite basic. There is typically a "home" page that provides your practice's location data, and perhaps a map, some images, and a few platitudes about how great your practice is, etc. There are likely other pages on the site, with content written to give the reader confidence in your practice. Typically, these pages provide additional information about several of your practice specialties. A "testimonials" page with comments from past patients, and a "contact us" page are characteristically included, as well.

If this describes your site, then we suggest an interesting exercise that might change what you believe about your website as a marketing tool. Print out the home page of your site, then find the sites of six of your top competitors. Print out their home pages, and lay out all of the pages on a table. See how similar they are? When we've done this exercise with clients, in most cases, there was so little difference amongst the websites that we could change the company name at the top of the home page to that of a competitor and not see a significant change in the page content.

Why is that a problem? If a prospective client is looking for what you offer online, and all of the websites are essentially the same, what is the primary point of differentiation between the companies? *Price.* If everyone looks the same, then all the client is interested in is getting the lowest price.

As a consumer, most of the time one isn't necessarily aware of the quality differences between two services, the necessity for having a reliable service team after the sale, or the medical or legal "jargon" that is common in your practice—one doesn't even know what questions to ask.

That ignorance is your fault! That's right! As the

professional practitioner, you have failed, with your "pretty brochure" website, to offer a value proposition strong enough to convert that consumer from "who is the cheapest?" to "where can I get the best value, highest level of service, and top-quality care or representation?"

The second style of website is commonly referred to as an "E-commerce" website. An E-commerce site is a fully functional online store that allows you to sell products and services. This type of site is applicable primarily to the retail world and is rarely used in professional practices. An exception might be a chiropractor who offers a line of vitamins and supplements that can be purchased online.

Third is a "Blog" site. Blogs are a great client-relations tool for practices, and they make great online journals for personal use. Having a blog, and uploading fresh content on a regular basis, is a powerful marketing strategy for any practice that enjoys repeat visits from its client base. Your blog shares your personality and that of your business, it keeps clients involved with your practice, and it helps you maintain "top of mind" awareness with them.

The challenge of starting either a blog page on your business website or a standalone blog is that it becomes an animal that requires constant feeding. You must upload fresh content on a regular basis. Depending on the type of practice you have, this can be a once-a-month commitment or as frequently as several times per week. No matter what schedule you decide is appropriate for you, someone has to create that content and upload it on that schedule. For busy practitioners, this can be challenging.

Finally, the fourth style of online presence is called a "Lead Generation" or lead gen website. This is a site where the content is focused on the prospective client and their needs and questions. It has a headline directed towards the conversation in the mind of the typical prospective client. A lead gen site always offers free information, usually in the form of a report or study, which has a perceived value for the prospect—enough value that they are willing to give their email address to get the information. Once you have their email address, then you can use an auto-responder to stay in touch with them, giving more valuable answers to questions they may not even know to ask. This creates the image of you as the expert, and someone they will want to trust with their business.

Here is an example of a lead gen site you can look at. See how it compares to your company site:

www.terrellroofing.com

Notice the differences? While the company name and logo are at the top of the page, most people are immediately drawn to the headline about forty years of local experience. That is one of the value propositions of this company, their experience in the local market. As your eye takes you to the right side of the page, you see the offer to subscribe to their newsletter. Also, there are three mini-headlines that are easily read, describing their commercial and residential roofing services and siding products. Additionally, links to the other pages of the site with more information about the company (and testimonials), more services, videos, and the company blog are easily found across the top of the home page.

As you scroll down the home page, there is a video featuring the owner, a listing of various services, a call to action, and a link to a social media site. Finally, at the bottom of the page, there is a reference to their 12,000 customers served, as well as an offer for a free gift card with an estimate.

Following are links to some similarly designed sites from other business categories. What do they have in common? Each has a clearly stated value proposition, is graphically appealing, includes only limited written copy on the home page, has an offer that is easily found, and the site offers value to the prospective customer.

www.optomsecurity.com
www.callisterandassociates.com
www.treasurevalleyfamilydentistry.com

Why does this strategy of building a website work so well?

To properly answer that question, let us share with you the concept of the "Educational Spectrum." Think back over the last year or so to the patients you have worked with. How did they come to you? Were they from one of your marketing channels, or as a referral from another past patient? These are the two most likely scenarios. Do you suppose that very many of your recent patients woke up one morning and said to themselves, "I think I'll go find a new (your service) today?" Not likely. In fact, most of them spent some time looking on the internet for advice, then probably asked a friend or coworker for a recommendation.

In other words, they invested some time educating themselves before making a commitment to meeting you and purchasing the service you offer. That process is called the educational spectrum.

To better understand this concept, visualize a line with numbers from one through ten along its length. This line represents all of the people who live in the city or market area where you offer your services.

| 1 | 5 | 10 |

The people at the far left, numbers one and two, will never need your service at any time and are not prospects. For whatever reason, they will never be candidates for your offer. The "tens" at the other end are your past clients who think you have the best company ever. They are tremendously pleased with the job you did for them, refer others to you, and have become "raving fans" of your practice.

Everyone in between, the threes through the nines, are prospects who have a reason for doing business with you or one of your competitors. As they start the process of learning about what you offer, we say that they are "stepping onto the educational spectrum." That means they are beginning to ask the questions and do the research that will enable them to make an informed buying decision.

As a prospective client moves towards the right side of this continuum, they are closer to actually pulling out their credit card and making a buying decision. Think about it. When someone is an eight or a nine, what is their primary motivation? If you said price, you are correct. By the time a prospect gets to that point on the education spectrum, they are already committed to engaging the service and are really just price-shopping. You may have heard the expression "low-hanging fruit." It refers to these people who are waving their credit card in the air and are ready to buy.

Why? Why do you want to spend your time talking with prospective clients who are focused on getting the lowest price? Even if you have a great "inside reality" and offer a much better product and service, this buyer's "outside perception" is that price is the primary point of differentiation.

What if you could begin a conversation with that prospect when they are still a three, four, or five on the educational spectrum, just as they are beginning to do their research for a new family dentist? What if you had the opportunity to share with them the great inside reality of your practice—the value proposition that sets you apart from your competition and makes you worth this client's business, even if your price is higher?

That is the value of a lead generation website. Most people who begin to research a topic will go to the internet. They will type into their browser something like, "chiropractor Sacramento" or "orthodontist Miami" and begin to scan through the first two pages. (According to Google, statistically less than 10 percent of internet searches go past page two.)

This potential client may see a pay-per-click ad and select it. If you are fortunate, your organic website listing is on those first two pages. You may have one or more properly optimized videos that show on these pages and take the shopper to your site through a link. Maybe you are listed in the Maps section, and they can link to you that way. Whatever the path, the client identifies several companies and clicks through to the practice websites. Do you remember the discussion about how everyone's brochure site looks the same, and how that steers a prospective client to conclude that all practices are essentially the same? In that scenario, price becomes their only concern.

If you have a lead gen website, it will immediately stand out as different, for several reasons. First, it includes a headline relevant to someone thinking about buying what you offer. Instead of the "we're the best" clichés that your competitors offer, you actually join the conversation that is in the mind of the prospective client by offering valuable information that answers their questions. You do that by offering to send them a report that elaborates on what they want or need to know about your product/service.

In addition to the report, you might have other offers that give a prospect the opportunity to move to the next step in the educational spectrum in a way that is comfortable for them. Instead of directing them to "call for an appointment" like everyone else, you might offer a recorded message detailing the "Seven Questions to Ask before Hiring a Business Attorney." As they jump around on your website, there can be other offers; for example, a report on "Working with Your Insurance Company to Minimize Your Out-of-Pocket Expense for Dental Implants."

To obtain this valuable information, they trade their email address, and you send them the report. Now you have permission to communicate with them via email. Should you then send them sales messages? *NO!* You want to continue to share your knowledge through valuable tips and links to social verification about you and your firm. You are building the "know-like-trust" relationship that will make certain your prospective client includes you when they are ready to talk with a practitioner.

What the prospect experiences when coming to your lead gen site is a wealth of information, answers to questions, and more importantly, answers to the questions they didn't know to ask. They will see testimonials from past patients, before-and-after photos (if appropriate), detailed descriptions of practice specialties, and a way to contact you. What they won't experience is every page asking them to call for an appointment. The prospective patient can move along at their own pace.

The result is that when they are ready to actually schedule appointments to "audition" the professional they need, your practice is included in that list. Why? You have created a relationship with them through the communication you've had over the time they were progressing along the education spectrum.

A lead generation website requires a different thought process for a practice owner. Most of us seem to have learned about marketing by looking at the Yellow Pages—at least that is what we think when we see many business websites. At the top are the company name and maybe a slogan (usually a trite platitude). Following that is a list of services, similar to a menu board at the deli. At the end is a call to action, something like "call for an appointment," and a phone number in bold type.

Really? Think about it. When you see an advertisement like that, do you ever stop and read it? We mean *actually read* all of the copy and think to yourself, "Hmmm, maybe I should call them." Almost never! Why? Because the ad doesn't say anything about what you, as their potential patient, are interested in—your "hot buttons." *The ad is all about the practice and nothing about the prospect.*

When we work with a client to help them enhance their marketing, we ask them to complete several exercises. A detailed explanation of each of these is beyond the scope of this chapter, but let us give you a quick overview designed to help make you a better writer of advertising copy.

Effective copy speaks to the needs of the prospective patient—it is focused on the conversation in their mind about your product or service. Your prospect truly doesn't care if you've been in business since 1876 and have the greatest group of employees since George Washington picked his first Cabinet. What that prospective client cares about is having their personal needs met. If, in your advertising, you can demonstrate your ability to do that, then you have a chance to capture their attention, trust, and eventually, their business.

So how *do* you do that?

It is simple—you ask them. When we work with a client, we obtain a list of recent patients and interview them, asking a series of fourteen question designed to help us uncover their real motivations. Here are four of the most important discovery questions; we encourage you to have this type of conversation with recent patients of your practice.

1.   Under what circumstances does the typical prospective patient begin to think about your service?

2.   What things are important to your prospects when buying your service?

3.   What are the relevant and important issues that a potential clients need to be aware of when making a decision about your service?

All three of these questions are *strategic,* that is, they focus on John Smith's desires—his "hot buttons." Put in modern terms, you might think of it as "which keywords a prospective client would use when they search on Google for a professional in your field." Don't assume that you know the answer to that question. Even for a task as simple as finding a dentist, people will use a variety of search terms.

4.   Where did the prospect look for a (your practice specialty)? That is, how did they find you and call for information? This question is *tactical.* Once you know where most of your customers are looking—and the search terms they are using—you will know where to invest your marketing budget for the highest return.

Many times when we begin this exercise, it is the first time our client has actually stopped and thought about what might be important to their prospect. It can be a very revealing experience! As business owners, most of us are so focused on what we offer that we rarely stop and think about how a prospective client views or experiences our company and our team. It can be sobering to realize how much money we have left on the table over the time we've been in business because of this lack of awareness.

We encourage you to spend some quiet time thinking about these questions and write down your thoughts. Ask your key employees to do the same and compare your answers. This, too, can be a very revealing experience!

Writing copy for a lead gen website and your other marketing activities is going to require a new way of thinking, and we want to share with you what we call the "Marketing Equation." This idea is based on the belief that marketing is science, not art. By understanding more about our client, seeing the world through their eyes, we can craft our advertising statements to speak to the conversation in their mind and win the right to talk further with them.

The marketing equation has four components. As we describe them, think about an advertisement you will be writing for your practice. It could be a flyer, a newspaper ad, the homepage of your website, or the ad you are going to put on a postcard. Here are the components:

1.	<u>Interrupt</u>—causes qualified prospects to pay attention to your marketing. Think of this as the headline for your advertisement. It must be based on the hot buttons that are important to your prospect. It should answer one or more of the discovery questions you thought through earlier. Here are some hints:

- Your company name is not a hot-button headline for your prospect. DO NOT put it at the top of your advertisements.
- No "false betas." A false beta is an interrupt that has no relevance to your company or product. For example, putting a Ferrari in your chiropractic practice ad. While you will catch the eye of many people, once they realize the image has no congruence with your service, they will move on and never read the rest of your marketing piece.
- A question can be a good interrupt, but it is difficult to phrase in broad enough terms to interrupt a large cross-section of the readership. It is better to make a declarative statement.

2.	<u>Engage</u>—think of this as a sub-headline. In effect, what you are saying to your reader is that, "If you continue to read, there is information coming that will help in your decision-making process about my practice."

74

3. Educate—identify important issues for the prospect and demonstrate how you solve them. For most marketing campaigns, bullet points are a great way to do this. On your website you can use more copy, but keep it focused on the prospect.

4. Offer—give them a low-risk way to take the next step in the decision-making process. You want to make your prospective client feel like they're in charge. The next step may be coming into your office, but it could also be requesting a report or visiting a web page. Too often, we try to jump from initially meeting a prospect to handing them a contract and asking for their signature. Just like when you were dating, the sales process requires a time of wooing. This is particularly true in highly competitive marketplaces, like most professional practices experience.

Here is one example of how this works in a "real world" setting—writing an advertisement to go on a postcard. We will make this generic, so you can visualize a variety of practices using the format.

First is the Interrupt (headline). On the front side of the card, I would feature a full-color image, maybe a person in a white lab coat looking at a clipboard. Over the top of the photo is this Interrupt (headline):

3 Critical Questions to Ask a Chiropractor

Second, try to Engage (sub-headline). How about something like:

Do You Know What They Are?

With just those few words, you have the attention of anyone who has been thinking about finding a chiropractor. We still haven't told them the name of our company, or any of the great slogans we've come up with that describe how wonderful we are. But...right now they are turning over the postcard to learn more, and that's the whole point!

Third, attempt to Educate. What are those "3 Critical Questions"? This is where we tell them. Because we only have part of a postcard to do so, bullet points are the logical way to do it. What is contained in the bullet points? We speak directly to the issues in the mind of the prospective patient we identified in the discovery questions exercise. For example:

- Expertise. (Make a few-word statement about the level of education and experience a prospect should expect. Obviously you must meet this criteria).
- Pain Relief. (Briefly address the primary reason most people would call— physical pain—and your process to alleviate it.)

- Patient Experience. (What you do to make the patient feel comfortable working with you.

Fourth is the Offer. Here is where you place your company name and tell the prospect the specific next step you want them to take.

XYZ Chiropractic Clinic
Go to www.xyzreport.com to get your free report and see how We Stack Up

The point of this exercise was to give you an example of an ad that follows the marketing equation; an ad that actually addresses the needs of your prospects. When you think about it, it is easier to structure an ad like this than to try to cram in a lot of generalities that really don't tell your prospect anything.

How does this apply to a website? Follow the same formula. The only exception we make when designing a home page, is that we *do* put the company name near the top of the page. It is in smaller type than what you usually see, and it is secondary to the headline and offer that always appear near the top of the screen. Other than that, the steps are exactly the same.

The marketing equation applies to your pay-per-click ads, landing pages, flyers— every advertising piece you create should follow this formula!

To summarize, a lead generation website is focused on the customer and their needs, not your company. It is not an "electronic brochure" that offers a list of features you believe are important, without sharing the benefit to your patient of each of those features. It always offers an easy way for the prospect to take the next step along the education spectrum, at a pace that is comfortable for them. That is typically in the form of a free report offering information that is valuable to the prospect.

Your lead gen site will include secondary pages for testimonials, photos, information about your practice and team members; the traditional pages that people who dig deeply into your site expect. The difference is that these, too, are written to help the customer get to know your inside reality in a way that is meaningful to them.

WHAT TO DO NOW:

1. If you want an effective lead gen site, you are going to have to be proactive with the graphics person and site designer you work with. Most designers are used to creating "brochure" sites, and they don't understand the why and how of building a site that is truly a marketing tool and not just "pretty."

We suggest you make a detailed sketch of how you want your home page to look, along with the overall appearance of the rest of the pages. If you are creating a WordPress site, work with your designer to find a theme that easily facilitates this. (Our preference is a three-column theme, as it offers a lot of flexibility for individual page construction. There are many choices—look for one that has been created for professional practices.)

2. What is the offer on your home page going to be? We suggest a free report with a title that speaks directly to the interests of the prospective customer. Some examples of reports we've done are:

"6 Things Your Insurance Company Won't Tell You about Medical Testing"

"10 Easy Things You Can Do at Home to Ease Back Pain"

"7 Questions to Ask a Personal Injury Attorney before Giving Them Your Case"

Can you see how each of these speaks to the conversation in the mind of someone considering the purchase of a specific service? Obviously, the report should help the prospect understand how your practice meets all of the criteria established in the report. It is not a blatant "commercial" for your company, but it should put questions in the mind of the prospect that you can answer positively as they come to you after reading.

Write the report(s) and identify what is needed for any other offers you might make on the site. Make the reports graphically appealing—don't just send them a Word document. Hire a graphics person to design an appropriate cover, and include images, charts, and other graphics in the report as appropriate.

3. One of the reasons you offer the free report is to capture the prospect's email address. This allows you to send them interesting and valuable information over a short period of time via email. This further solidifies you as an expert who is focused on offering value, not just asking for an appointment.

The tool you'll need to manage this is called an auto-responder. It is a software program that allows you to create a series of emails, which are delivered on a preprogrammed schedule you determine. Your auto-responder system will also "host" your free report and deliver automatically when someone fills out the form on your website.

There are at least a dozen auto-responder companies to choose from. We have used several of them and find an auto-responder to be a valuable tool for business marketing. Three that are easy to learn and have a low monthly cost are:

www.aweber.com	Very popular in marketplace
www.getresponse.com	We currently use at Alchemy
www.mailchimp.com	Lowest cost system we know of

Choose an auto-responder program for your company. Write a series of six to eight, short, information-packed emails that can be delivered over a period of fourteen to twenty days after a prospect orders your report. Upload your report to the auto-responder, and create the form code your web designer will need to put the opt-in form on your site.

Most web designers will have experience with these steps and can help you complete them. Of course, you'll want to write the report and email copy yourself.

4. Continue to market your lead gen website in all of your other marketing pieces. If you have not yet started a reputation marketing program for your company, consider doing so quickly as this will help your site's organic positioning with the search engines.

CONCLUSION

We hope that you understand the importance of having a website for your business. More important, is that it is a lead generation site.

There are two other concepts we shared in this chapter that are absolutely critical to the long-term success of any marketing you do for your practice. One is the educational spectrum and the importance of building a relationship with your prospects early in their process of learning about what you offer. Unless you are in the business of selling a low-priced "commodity" product that people buy without a lot of reflection, this concept will change your business! Any medical or professional services firm should evaluate their current marketing campaigns in light of this idea for building relationships before the sale, to encourage the sale.

The other important concept is the model of creating marketing pieces and advertising copy that follows the marketing equation. This may be the single-most important idea that we share with you in this book. If you implement this way of thinking in your marketing, it will dramatically improve the effectiveness of all your communication with prospects.

These concepts are so important that, if you aren't confident about how to apply them for your company and want to talk about them, we offer Gordon's phone number, 505-720-2647, to assist you. That is a cell phone, so if he doesn't pick up it means he is with someone. Leave a message and why you're calling, and he will get back with you as soon as possible. We live in the U.S., in the Mountain Time zone, so please don't call in the middle of the night!

Chapter Four

Retargeting: Online "Stalking"—But in A Good Way

It doesn't matter how attractive, interactive, or appealing your website might be; the reality is that 98 percent of your visitors will leave without taking any action (according to HubSpot, October 2015). Retargeting is a strategy to help you bring those people back to your site.

Here is the process. A prospective client comes to your website or visits you on a mobile app; they look around for awhile, but then leave without converting to the next step you offer. Sometime later, they are back online, either at their desk or on their mobile device. They see ads for your company, usually displayed in the form of banners. Your ad captures their interest enough that they will click on the banner. This returns them to your site, where they convert and become loyal customers.

This chapter contains an overview of this powerful and easy-to-implement business growth strategy. We will expand on the definition of retargeting and how it works, give you two reasons why you should consider implementing a retargeting program, and detail some best practices for doing just that.

First, a clarification. In another chapter, we discuss the strategy of real-time bidding (RTB). As you read that chapter, you might recognize that retargeting is one type of real-time bidding; in fact, it is the most basic form of RTB. However, RTB is a multi-dimensional application of banner ads to specific markets. It is proactive in that you can target prospects who have not visited your website. Retargeting is reactive; you place your message in front of someone who has already been to your site.

Another, more important difference is that RTB requires you to enlist the help of a demand-side platform provider and a much larger budget. Retargeting is something you can implement on your own, with just a few dollars to invest.

Another important distinction to understand, especially for those who have invested in a pay-per-click campaign in the past, is that with PPC, you pay every time a prospect clicks on your ad. In a retargeting campaign, you pay per "impression," meaning every time your banner is displayed to a prospect. Your cost is calculated based on 1,000 impressions, and expressed as "CPM," cost-per- (1,000) impressions.

While it seems like the expense could add up quickly, the reality is that retargeting is less costly than PPC. We have clients who spend between $15 and $20 per click, but only $7 CPM.

Retargeting can be most beneficial. If you look at the progression a prospective client goes through, ultimately to become your client, you can see that it almost always is a multi-step process. Only rarely does someone visit your site for the first time and become a client at that point. Google did a study on the typical sales-conversion funnel, finding that it can take as many as thirty steps for a prospect to become a client.

Retargeting helps you tackle this problem head-on. It allows you to target and serve ads only to people who have previously visited your website, used your mobile app, or in some cases, visited and bought something from a physical retail location. This means you can be very strategic and efficient about who you're reaching and where you're spending your marketing budget.

Why should you consider a retargeting campaign for your professional practice? There are two reasons. First, it is a direct-response marketing technique with a high return on investment. In the competitive, and often extended, time cycle to go from prospect to client, retargeting is the most direct way to reconnect with high-value prospects. It gives you a mechanism to recapture their attention with an effective and compelling message, moving them along in your sales funnel.

The second reason is "brand awareness." We don't often suggest that a small business consider the financial investment necessary to create a significant "brand" in their marketplace. With a well-designed retargeting campaign, you are subtly reaching prospects in your community and, by virtue of multiple impressions, "branding" your business in their minds. According to Comscore, retargeting campaigns led to a 1,046 percent increase in branded search, and a 726 percent lift in site visits after four weeks of ad exposure. Retargeting just might be the most cost-efficient branding strategy available.

We briefly introduced you to the mechanics of retargeting at the start of this chapter. In more detail, there is a difference between "desktop" and "mobile" devices; while the process is similar, the technology to implement retargeting is different between the two.

Retargeting on desktop devices relies on the use of tracking tags and cookies. To implement a program, you would place a snippet of JavaScript code called a tracking tag into your website's source code. This tracking tag puts an anonymous "cookie" in the browser of everyone who visits your website. This cookie enables you to identify audiences based on their browsing behavior. The data captured is not specific to the individual visitor, as no personal information is retained.

Depending on the flow of traffic to your website, it can take some time to develop a critical mass of visitor data that can be segmented for unique offers.

Mobile retargeting has been gaining rapidly in popularity. A recent issue of *Digital Marketer* projected that, at some point later in 2016, the total ad spend for mobile retargeting will exceed desktop-spend for the first time. The challenge for business owners is that the data is less reliable, since tablets and mobile devices do not allow for the placement of third-party cookies. So how does retargeting occur without cookies? Two methods have been developed—probabilistic matching and deterministic matching.

Probabilistic matching involves the collection of data from mobile users: IP, location data, device and browser type, etc. Algorithms have been developed to evaluate thousands of data points and make correlations between them. While accuracy has been increasing, this method is still less than 70 percent accurate—it is more of a "best guess" method.

Deterministic matching ties devices together, using a mix of user and device IDs. This might include Twitter and Facebook accounts, an email address, and a customer ID. While this method is more accurate, the data pool is significantly smaller.

For the professional practice manager who wants to implement a retargeting campaign themselves, the best option is to concentrate on the desktop pixel placement and focus on regenerating interest from website visitors. If you decide to hire a third-party firm to manage your retargeting, then talk with them about mobile programs they might have available.

Strategies for Retargeting Campaigns

Some "best practices" for managing your retargeting campaigns include:

1. Place the site-tracking tag on every page of your website. Even if you plan to start small and retarget a single audience, by tagging all pages at the beginning, you will save a lot of time later. Additionally, if you have a product feed, connect it to your retargeting platform. This will enable you to retarget visitors based on the specific product(s) they view.

2. Run campaigns across multiple channels. This means don't rely on just Google or just Facebook. Even the most popular websites represent only a fraction of the typical person's online activity. The best opportunity for maximizing conversions is to reach out to your visitors across as many sites and channels as possible.

3. <u>Be aware of the seasonal impact of competition on your campaigns</u>. You will want to increase your bids accordingly. The obvious example is during the holidays when retail advertising is at its peak. If you keep your bids at the same level as other times of the year, your ads will not be displayed with the same frequency due to the increased number of companies in the marketplace. As a general rule of thumb, increase your CPM bid by at least 50 percent during these months to ensure that you're staying in front of your desired customers.

4. <u>Retarget your landing pages</u>. If you are an aggressive marketer with multiple sales funnels, you have various landing pages to which you drive traffic. While these pages will generally have a higher conversion rate than your main website, not everyone will move forward as you hope. Retargeting these visitors promptly and frequently will increase your responses.

5. <u>Create appealing ads that are focused on the interests of your prospect</u>. The most sophisticated internet campaign will fall flat if your creatives do not contain a clear and targeted message. How to do that? Be relevant; consider your audience's interests. Be concise, as space is at a premium. Be compelling, with bold imagery and a strong call to action.

The final component of your retargeting campaign is to

optimize performance and increase your return on investment. Launching a campaign is relatively easy, but optimizing those campaigns can be challenging, and it is not always clear how to begin. Following are some suggestions for how to get underway.

- First, block or blacklist poorly performing sites. Start out by looking back at a month's data. If there are sites displaying your banners that are not meeting conversion goals, simply block or blacklist them. It is okay to be a little ruthless at the beginning; you can go back and unblock a site if you want to collect more data.

- Second, analyze and optimize your look-back window. This is the amount of time you want to continue to target a visitor. As an example, if your look-back window is ten days, your campaigns will target anyone who has visited your website within the last ten days.

  This process takes some judgment. The longer the look-back window, the larger your audience. The negative to this is that visitors to your site from farther back in time are less likely to respond to your ads over time. You also will want to analyze your typical sales cycle, to determine the time period when the purchase life cycle most often resolves. What is the time between someone's first visit and when they purchase? What is the time frame when 80 percent of purchases have been completed? It makes sense to optimize your look-back window to a similar time frame.

- Third, set frequency caps. How often do you want someone to see your ad? It is a delicate balance; too many exposures can cause prospective clients to become annoyed with your product and brand. Automated retargeting systems will manage this for you, but you will need to monitor and determine the best level of exposure for your product or service.

Fourth, don't rely only on clicks as a measure of campaign success. Many practice managers, particularly those who have used PPC advertising, assume that if an ad is not getting clicks, it is a defective ad. That is not necessarily the case with retargeting. According to Google, people do not click on banner ads like they do paid ads on the search result page. In fact, Google studies indicate an average click through rate of just .11 percent.

There is a phenomenon of online display advertising referred to as "view-through attribution." This describes the behavior of the person who sees your banner ad, maybe several times, but never clicks it. They later return to your website and convert to a client. Though difficult to measure, this increased awareness of your product and/or brand (called "incremental lift") can be attributed to banner advertising.

The only way to quantify this is to conduct a series of A/B split tests of your ads, while closely monitoring the overall conversion rate within your marketing funnels. These tests should run for at least two look-back windows.

WHAT TO DO NOW:

1. Decide if you want to implement a retargeting campaign, and if you are going to do it yourself or hire a management company.

2. If you want to control your own campaigns, begin by following the directions Google offers for creating retargeting (they call it "remarketing") within their platform. This will give you a basic knowledge of how to create and monitor a campaign.

3. Have your graphics person design several iterations of your ads so they can be tested. Continue to identify your best ads through testing and give them additional exposure.

4. When you're ready, expand your campaign to other platforms; for example, Facebook.

CONCLUSION

Retargeting is an incredibly powerful tool for turning someone just passing through your website into a loyal patient. It allows you to re-engage with your best targets and prospects. Further, it enables you to provide added value with personalized and engaging content. Retargeting should be considered as a valuable addition to your outbound marketing toolkit.

Chapter Five

Pay-Per-Click—The Best Way to Get on Page One of the Search Engines

Paid search engine advertising has become an almost-universal marketing strategy, especially since the fall of 2015. During August, September, and October of that year, Google implemented a significant change in the search engine results pages. The change was on page one, where we used to see what were called "maps listings." There were seven listings for most searches, thus the common name for this highly coveted, page-one real estate: the "seven-pack."

A result of this modification to the site-display formula is that instead of up to seven practices being listed for most searches, there are now just three. A "dropdown" link can be clicked to reveal more businesses, but it is not obvious.

There is little doubt that the purpose of this change was to drive more practice owners to pay for advertising: pay-per-click. With the latest version of the search engine algorithm, there is only one way to guarantee visibility on the top two pages of search results—that is to buy advertising.

However, don't assume that just because you are willing to buy ads that you will get clicks from prospective clients. If not managed correctly, pay-per-click advertising can be one of the biggest wastes of your valuable marketing budget. Even those companies that retain the services of a paid advertising manager may not be achieving the best return on investment (ROI). As the practice owner, if you aren't conversant with how to correctly set up and monitor a paid advertising campaign, how will you know?

In this chapter, we will answer several frequently asked questions we encounter when talking with practice owners and managing partners about paid searches. These include:

- What is paid search advertising?
- What are the benefits of using paid search for a professional practice in my niche?
- How do I begin if I want to start a paid advertising campaign?
- What is a quality score, and how is it calculated?
- How do I write an effective ad?
- Why do I need landing pages?
- What are the top five mistakes to avoid in my paid search campaigns?
- Can I hire someone to manage this for me? How do I do that?

Our purpose in this chapter is to give you enough information so that you know the right questions to ask, whether you decide to have someone on your team supervise your paid-ad campaigns or you retain the services of an outside company. Keep in mind that search engine advertising is dynamic—change is the rule and not the exception. If you decide to invest a sizeable percentage of your marketing budget in paid search, you must also commit to a consistent program of testing and learning.

What is Paid Search Advertising?

For this discussion, we refer to all types of paid search advertising using the acronym "PPC." PPC stands for *pay-per-click,* and it refers to the type of search engine marketing in which an advertiser pays a fee each time one of their ads is clicked. Essentially, PPC is a way of buying visits to your site, rather than attempting to "earn" those visits organically.

Most paid search is done using the three major search engines: Google, Bing, and Yahoo. For simplicity's sake, we will use "Google" as a generic reference to these search engines. (Google currently controls 70 percent of the search market.)

A PPC advertising program is quite simple to begin. You create an account with the search engines—an "AdWords" account, as referred to by Google; this account is funded through your credit card. Then, you place an advertisement that is tied to the keywords that you believe your prospects will search. Every time your ad is clicked, sending a visitor to your website, you have to pay the search engine a small fee. When PPC is working correctly, the fee is trivial, because *the visit is worth more than what you pay for it*. In other words, if you pay $136 for a click, but the click results in a $9,000 cosmetic surgery patient, then you've made a hefty profit and return on that advertising investment.

A lot goes into building a winning PPC campaign: researching and selecting the right keywords, organizing those keywords into well-structured campaigns and ad groups, and setting up PPC landing pages that are optimized for conversions. Search engines reward advertisers who create relevant, intelligently targeted pay-per-click campaigns by charging them less for ad clicks. If your ads and landing pages are useful and satisfying to users, Google charges you less per click, leading to higher profits for your business.

PPC marketing is not limited to the search engines. Facebook now accepts ads, and in many ways, its program is superior to that offered by Google. First,

Facebook ad costs are generally lower than a corresponding ad on Google, Bing, or Yahoo. Second, because Facebook collects so much data on its users, you can be quite specific to whom you display your ad. Third, the Facebook dashboard for ad management is quite intuitive and easy to use. Fourth, split-testing of your ads (comparing the results of one ad against another) is less complicated. Finally, because Facebook allows you to direct where your ad is placed, there is not the "quality score" challenge that is part of advertising on the search engines.

The downside of advertising on Facebook is that people shopping for professional services might not think to go to Facebook to find what they want. Your Facebook ad must interrupt the prospect while they are on the site and lead them to a landing page that is compelling enough for them to call you. This is changing as Facebook accepts more ads and users become accustomed to seeing them. Still, at the time of this writing and for the foreseeable future, paid advertising for most companies will be on Google or another search engine.

What Are the Benefits of Using Paid Search for Your Practice?

PPC campaigns have numerous benefits, including:

measurability, payment for performance, timing, control, bidding, speed to market, and targeting.

Following are a few examples of how PPC can help you achieve specific practice goals:

Business Goals Examples

Generate new leads: Use PPC to obtain new prospects and gather information about their needs over time.

Drive new prospects to a distinct landing page on your website where they can sign up for a free demo or download a new report or free content.

Direct Sales: Drive new leads to a transaction page.

Build Brand Awareness: Use PPC to invite prospects to an event, either on- or offline, or to promote something newsworthy.

Assess Immediately: Use a true pay-for-performance marketing medium to allow you to quickly determine whether your campaign is profitable or not.

Some of the benefits of PPC for your practice include:

Measurable: With a proper tracking system in place, you know exactly where your prospects came from and the results.

Pay for performance: You only pay for actual clicks to your listing. If a user enters a search term, sees your site and clicks the listing, it is because s/he believes your listing will provide the info s/he wants.

Control what visitors see on your site: You can direct traffic to specific pages on your site. You should develop landing pages for each campaign—pages offering specific information and a strong call to action.

Excellent timing: You bid on the search terms/keywords used by your prospects when they are searching for info on the web.

Bid what a prospect is worth: You can input different bid amounts on keywords to reflect how valuable the leads are for you. For example, you may bid on a very specific phrase such as, "Family Dentist, Portland," and pay more for those clicks because they are more valuable to you than general keywords that may drive a greater volume of less-targeted traffic.

Limit spending: You choose a maximum bid level so that you only spend what those website visits are worth.

Speed to market: You can launch a paid search campaign as soon as your website is live, building immediate traffic that may take months to generate organically.

Develop targeted campaigns: You can develop very specific campaigns that include seasonality, regionality, and other factors that influence the purchasing decision.

How Do I Begin if I Want to Start a Paid Advertising Campaign?

In order to implement search-engine marketing best practices, it is important to understand who the players are in every PPC transaction. Most of us who have spent money on advertising in the past believe that we are a priority for the vendor of the ad space or airtime or whatever marketing venue we invested in. *That is not the case with PPC advertising*.

There are three interrelated entities in constant tension in any PPC account. Most AdWords users have a good understanding of the marketing channel from a micro-point of view, meaning how they get into and work on their personal account. What they might fail to understand is the conceptual framework of a PPC account, and the important relationships involved.

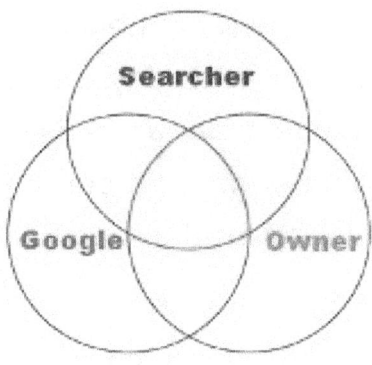

The three entities that are a part of every PPC transaction are the "Searcher," the AdWords account "Owner," and Google. Let's briefly analyze each of these, and then look at why a thorough understanding of this concept can save you thousands of dollars on your own campaigns.

<u>The Searcher</u>. This is the person looking for products and services online who types a search inquiry into the Google (or any search engine) search box. Google considers the searcher to be their primary customer, and constructs their algorithms to help searchers easily and accurately find what they are looking for. Part of helping the searcher is providing paid ads relevant to their keywords. Google has studied user eye movement and selection tendencies extensively, and it will "reward" well-written and properly structured PPC campaigns with better placement on the page and a lower cost-per-click.

While an advertiser is the source of cash flow, searchers

are the lifeblood of any search engine. Without its tens of millions of searches each day, Google would quickly wither up and die. As an advertiser, we can never assume that we are more important to the search engines than the searcher; the searcher controls the PPC world.

The Owner. This is the person who creates an AdWords account and uses the PPC marketing channel to sell a product or service to the searcher. The owner is also a customer of Google, but in the overall scheme of things, takes a back seat in terms of importance.

The search engines place a lot of emphasis on owners' compliance with detailed regulations that sometimes seem illogical from an advertising point of view. These rules are in place to protect the searcher from any owner misconduct or misleading advertising. Google will always err on the side of protecting the searcher. Therefore, the onus falls on the owner to comply with these policies and rules. Failure to do so may get an owner "slapped," or banned, from advertising on the Google platform.

The owner must learn to think like the potential searcher. What words is a searcher likely to type into the search bar to help them find your services? (Owners of an AdWords account have analysis tools that will help them know what words searchers are typing during their searches.) By incorporating those words into the "headline" of your ad, you enhance the experience for the searcher, and in the process, earn a higher "quality score" (QS) from the search engine. It is this quality score that determines where your ad is placed on the page, and the cost-per-click you pay.

The ongoing challenge for any advertiser (owner) using PPC is creating advertisements compelling enough for searchers to click, which also comply with Google's best practices. The advertiser is constantly testing to improve these ads, while, in the process, also lowering advertising costs.

<u>Google</u> (or any search engine). Google has two customers: the searcher and the owner. While Google wants both of its customers to be satisfied using the AdWords platform, it is also in business to make a profit. If you are new to paid search advertising and decide to open an AdWords account, you will find training provided by Google. However, if you carefully analyze the results of the suggested default settings for a PPC account, you will see that many are set up to help a PPC client spend more money.

As you develop a longer track record with Google as an advertiser, they will offer you ideas for how to utilize more of the platform's capabilities (*i.e.*, spend more money.) You may also be assigned a customer service rep who will contact you directly with suggestions and proposals. What you will never hear from Google are ideas about how you can spend less. They are a profit-driven company, and AdWords is their primary profit generator.

It falls to the owner to be aware of how to manage a campaign to generate the highest return on investment for dollars being spent on PPC. This must also be done while following the rules created to protect the searcher.

Failure to understand the "big picture" of PPC can cost you a great deal of money, and possibly even get you banned from the platform. Failure to "see" with the eyes of your prospect, adjusting your campaigns accordingly, can cause a total disconnect between you and your potential client.

For you as the owner, the goal of a well-run PPC campaign is to understand both the searcher and Google enough to maximize your results at the lowest possible cost. It is not a "set it and forget it" program.

The PPC Auction

The actual transaction of someone going to the search engine, typing in a query, and then being taken to a page that includes a variety of paid ads is a complicated "auction" process that occurs in milliseconds. Here's how it works:

The process begins with the searcher entering their inquiry terms. When they do that, Google looks at the available pool of advertisers and determines whether there will be an auction. If more than one advertiser is bidding on keywords that *Google deems relevant to the search query*, an auction is triggered. Keep in mind that keywords are not search queries. Specific keywords may be entered into auctions for a wide range of search queries, depending on the match type you have specified in your advertising account.

What gets entered into these auctions? Advertisers identify keywords they want to bid on, how much they are willing to spend, and create groupings of these keywords that are paired with ads. Google then enters the keyword that it deems to be most relevant from your account into the auction, with the maximum bid you've specified as well as the ad that is associated with that keyword.

Then, the confusion begins! Which ads appear on the page for the searcher, where do they show up on the page, and how much are you charged if your ad is selected? Actually, it is not that mysterious. Once you are entered into the auction, Google looks at two key factors to determine where your ad ranks: your maximum bid and your quality score. (We'll look at QS in detail later in this chapter.)

The auction formula is: Ad Rank (where your ad appears on the page) = Your Maximum Bid x Your Quality Score

The cost of your ad, if yours is selected by the searcher, is calculated as follows:

Your Price = Ad Rank of the Person below You / Your Quality Score + $0.01

It is commonly believed that the company that has the first ad at the top of the page is paying more than any other ad on the page. The second ad is paying the second-most, etc. As you can see from the formula, this is not necessarily true. The key variable is your quality score.

What Is a "Quality Score," and How Is It Calculated?

The secret to dramatically lowering your cost to acquire a new customer when using Google AdWords is simple: improve your quality score! Results of a study that used combined data from thousands of PPC campaigns run in the second half of 2015, representing just over $100 million in annual spend, can help us calculate just how much impact QS can have.

Here's the bottom line: for every QS point above the

average of five out of ten, your cost-per-acquisition (CPA) will drop by an average of 16 percent. Conversely, for every QS point below the average of five out of ten, your CPA will increase by 16 percent.

It is an oversimplification to state that the most important metric you should be looking at when managing your practice's AdWords advertising is quality score, but understanding the components of QS and focusing attention on improving it where you are able will have a definite impact on your ROI.

With Google's approach, QS matters because it represents the relevance of your ads to their customers' search queries. Calculating and assigning a QS to your advertising is one of the primary ways that Google maintains its status as the most-used search engine. This helps Google ensure that the ads Searchers are seeing are relevant to their inquiries. Both Bing and Yahoo have developed a similar metric to provide their users with the most relevant search results.

The bottom line is that quality score affects your account success. If your keyword-level QS is low, your keyword might not even be entered into an auction. That means your ad won't show at all, and you would have no chance to complete for business. If your QS is low, your ad rank will be low, driving less traffic to your site, at a higher price, and reducing your ROI.

There are actually seven different types of quality scores. "Seven types??" you might be asking. Most active users of PPC know about the QS associated with the individual keywords in their account, also known as the "visible level quality score." Fewer users are aware that Google calculates a variety of quality scores. How they are weighed with and against each other, and their combined impact on your account, remains shrouded in mystery. One thing is certain—that they were designed to help Google with one or both of its primary mandates: provide the best quality search experience for Google customers and do everything possible to maximize Google's income.

The seven distinct types of quality scores that we have been able to determine are described as follows.

1. <u>Account-Level Quality Score</u>. This score is the calculated result of the historical performance of all keywords and ads in an account. If you have a large number of low QS keywords and low click-through rate ads with poor historical performance in your account, your QS will remain low. This makes it difficult to introduce new keywords and ads, and they will start at this lower QS.

2. <u>Ad Group Quality Score</u>. This is a way to determine which areas you need to work on within a campaign. Let's say you have an ad group with a low keyword QS, but your overall average is a "seven." You have another ad group with an average of "four." This makes it clear where you should devote your attention; working on your lowest average QS areas first leads to a better ROI.

3. <u>Keyword-Level Quality Score</u>. This score is visible in your AdWords interface, and it is the QS that Google assigns to your keywords. It is a scale of one to ten, with "one" being poor and "ten" being fantastic. It is calculated by the performance of search queries that exactly match your keyword.

4. <u>Ad-Level Quality Score</u>. The individual ads that you are running in each of your ad groups will have a different click-through rate (CTR), which determines the overall ad-level QS. If you have a lot of low CTR ads in an ad group, this could be a contributing factor to a low QS, since AdWords considers all of your ads when calculating your scores.

5. <u>Landing Page Quality Score</u>. Google has three priorities for evaluating a landing page: relevant and original content, transparency, and

navigability. Google consciously attempts to force advertisers into making quality websites that its users will find useful and relevant.

6. <u>Display Network Quality Score</u>. Unless you are using the Google Display Network, this is not relevant. Professional practices would not normally use this network.

7. <u>Mobile Quality Score</u>. In the past twenty-four months, mobile searches have grown geometrically. One recent study indicated that 60 percent of all searches on Google originated from a mobile device. This trend begs the question: how does Google incorporate mobile into QS calculations? According to its own reports to tech partners, Google indicates that they do not discriminate between platforms—the calculation is exactly the same. However, their system does take into consideration for mobile search the distance between the user and business location, when available, by using the device location and location extensions data.

We have gone into more detail about quality scores than you might be interested in, but it is *that* important. Particularly for the practice manager who is tasked with managing their own campaign, a correct understanding of quality score can be the difference between a profitable program and one that is a waste of valuable time and money.

How Do I Write an Effective PPC Ad?

Writing ad copy for PPC can be a tough feat. The good news is you don't have to be a super-creative copywriter to whip up competitive ad text. In fact, following a pragmatic approach can be advantageous.

A few simple steps will help you to assess the competitive landscape and write ad copy that will stand out against your competitors, regardless of your ad rank.

1. Do competitive research. What are your competitors who use PPC saying in their ads? Most of the time, their "headlines" will be their company names or clichés about being the "best (business category) in (your city)." Unless you have also spent a great deal of money on radio, TV, or print ads over a period of years, most people looking for a business in your niche will not recognize your company name. Since everyone says they are the "best (business category)," that term is meaningless to a prospective client.

Also, realize that many of the paid ads will not be for your direct competitors. Companies like Home Advisors, Yellow Pages, Health Directories, Angie's List, Healthlinks, the Better Business Bureau, and other entities that offer consumers a listing of companies often spend a lot on PPC ads. Without anything else to go on, many seekers will choose one of these "data aggregators."

To stand out, your ad has to catch attention. Do you have a slogan or value proposition? Use it as a headline. We did some work for a roof repair company who had a great tagline: "Think you need a new roof? Think again!" It became a great headline for their PPC campaign ads. The point is, be different and stand out, and you'll get more clicks.

2. <u>Identify your differentiating characteristic</u>. Once you have assessed the competition, use your knowledge to become the leader of the pack. Consider your page-mates' ad copy and identify a differentiator that will make you stand out. This is your opportunity to sell yourself! Tell the prospective client why you are providing them a better product or deal than your competitors.

The difference might be your years in the marketplace, or that you achieved a top ranking from the BBB, or that your company was selected for an industry award—anything that might attract attention and prompt a searcher to read your advertisement.

3. <u>Include a call to action</u>. To complete your ad, include a call to action that gives your searchers an incentive to click. You can opt for the standard "call us now," but if you want to step it up a notch, consider a more creative alternative. If you have a high-profile past client, (with their permission) include something like "Coach Smith trusted his contract negotiation to us; you should too." Make an offer that gives something of value to a homeowner: "Free Family Oral Care kit for every new patient."

4. <u>Use ad extensions</u>. Extensions are a way to increase the size of your ad at no additional cost. Several types of extensions you can utilize include call extensions, site-link extensions, location extensions, offer extensions, and application extensions (for people using a tablet or mobile phone to search), among others.

5. <u>Watch Your Metrics</u>. Your ad may be complete, but you're not finished yet. Let it acquire a few impressions, and then assess your success! It is tough to predict the performance of a new ad, so ad-copy testing is critical. Often the ad copy you thought would win out ends up losing. There's no way to know what will work until you test ads against each other.

Why Do I Need Landing Pages?

A classic mistake that far too many practice owners make when starting a new PPC campaign is sending someone who clicks on their ad directly to their website, usually to the home page. "What's wrong with that?" you might be asking. While you may have an award-winning homepage designed by a well-known internet guru who charged you a lot of money, it may not be at all relevant to the reason someone is searching for you.

Your PPC ad is written for a specific response. It is crafted to speak to a specific need in the searcher's mind. Your website is a more general introduction to your company and all of its products/services. It may not immediately speak to the need in the mind of the prospect, whereas a landing page is a "single-page website" that does.

Why does someone need what you offer? What, specifically, are they looking for when they go to a search engine and type in their keywords? That is the question you want to answer for them immediately when they click on your ad. The way you do this is with a landing page. A landing page is just what it sounds like—an online page that specifically addresses the exact question the searcher is asking, which they "land on" when clicking your ad. Following is an example.

It is a sunny Saturday afternoon in late spring. Mrs. Jones is working in her kitchen when she hears a scream from the backyard. Her ten-year-old twin boys, Stan and Eric, have been playing quietly until now. As she rushes into the yard, she sees Stan screaming and holding his hands over his mouth. There is a lot of blood.

She quickly sorts through the yelling from both boys, and it is apparent that Stan has fallen off of the "fort" the boys had been building, landing chin-first on the concrete sidewalk. He has broken three teeth and lacerated his lower lip. After putting an ice bag on Stan's mouth, she runs to her computer and types in "24-hour emergency dentist."

That just happens to be a service your practice offers, and a keyword you use in one of your PPC ads. Mrs. Jones clicks on your ad and is directed to your home page. There she learns that you have been in practice for more than fifteen years, do a variety of dental procedures, accept most insurance plans, have two hygienists with lots of experience, and provide a whole lot of information that is not relevant to her immediate need: an emergency dentist. She gets frustrated and goes back to Google to find someone who answers her question.

When she clicked on your ad, if she had been taken to a landing page with just a few facts that were directly related to her question, you would have gotten the business. What did Mrs. Jones need in that moment? All she needed to see was a bold headline telling about 24/7 emergency service, and, in large type, the phone number you want her to call. Your practice name should also be on the page, but subordinate to the headline and phone number. Anything else is irrelevant to her needs at that moment. Does this make sense? **Think like your prospect!**

We call this strategy "One-Decision Marketing," because it is focused on helping a prospect make the one decision that is most relevant to them at that time. There is another advantage to using landing pages. Recall that Google's primary interest is ensuring that all of its search customers find what they need quickly and easily. The Google algorithms track search behavior and grade your ads and site based on how people react to them. In Mrs. Jones' example, if she had clicked on your ad, gone to a landing page and stopped her search, Google would assume that she found exactly what she needed. Kudos to you! However, because she went back and searched again, it is obvious she didn't get what she needed from your site. Not good! Your Quality Score is affected by her search behavior.

When we explain this to prospects and clients, a common question is, "Does that mean I need a landing page for each ad I run?" A landing page in not needed for each individual ad, but is necessary for each product or service you are marketing. You may have several ads—and each ad has specific keywords and, therefore, a specific want or need it is addressing—but are all focused on bringing prospects to a particular product or service. These ads should all be directed to a specific landing page so that a prospective patient has their immediate questions answered.

Put another way, in your dental practice you perform oral exams and fix cavities; yet you also do teeth whitening, root canals, implants, and bridge work. Each of these areas of specialization might have three or five or even more keyword phrases that are commonly typed in by searchers. Each of the keyword phrases can have one or more specific ads ("more" because you are constantly testing to improve your results). All of the ads will link to one landing page that has relevant information to that specific specialty of your practice, including a clear call to action so the searcher knows exactly what you want them to do next.

If you are just sending prospects to your home page, you are losing business as well as hurting your quality score. This costs you money!

Generally, your landing pages should be substantially different in content and style from a regular web page.

This is because they are built around different goals. Web pages may be built to rank organically, to inform, to entertain, and sometimes to sell. Landing pages are almost always intended to sell.

There Are (at Least) Five Pay-Per-Click Mistakes That Could Be Costing You Money

If you currently have active PPC campaigns as a part of your marketing spend each month, evaluate whether you are committing any of these "PPC sins."

1. Trusting the "default" setting in your AdWords account. If you read the earlier portion of this chapter, you understand that while Google is in the business of providing services to you as an advertiser, their primary motivation is to make the maximum profit they can from every account. There is nothing wrong with that, but you don't want to spend your money without extracting the maximum ROI possible.

Here's the Rule: It's your money—Maximize your return on investment!

Many PPC users do not evaluate just how the default settings in AdWords can impact their expenses. It is important to turn off any setting that will not optimize your ad spend. For example, the default setting is "on" for "content network." This means that your ads will be shown on sites like About.com and The New York Times, and you will pay for any curious viewers who click, whether they have an interest in, or ability to use, your service or not.

Will advertising in those venues help you sell your products or services? In most cases, no. You want your ads to show up for people who are directly searching for what you offer—we call this your "search network"—and not on secondary and even tertiary sites.

2. Confusing "clicks" with profits. It is imperative to know about conversion metrics and the importance of closely monitoring the statistics for each ad that you have running. Peter Drucker, the "man who invented management," once said, "What gets measured, gets managed." That is so true when it comes to pay-per-click. There are quite a few variables, and here are some suggestions to improve your results.

Here's the Rule: "Click through" is good... "Conversion" is better!

The most obvious measure of a PPC campaign is the percentage of time that a searcher will click on your ad. If you get one click for every 2,500 times your ad is displayed, you have a low click-through rate. If you're getting one for every five times—you're a genius! However, keep in mind that the click-through rate is useless, by itself. It will have a significant impact on the cost of your campaign, as you are paying per click, but it tells you nothing about the benefits you get in return.

The bottom line in any PPC campaign is how well the ad spend generates income. Every decision you make in any campaign should be focused on getting customers to spend money with you, not just to click on the ad. Potentially, an ad that is generating a huge number of clicks should be pulled because those prospects are not converting to customers. By the way, this same evaluation should be done for each keyword you choose to bid on.

One of the biggest advantages to online advertising is the ability to calculate your ROI. The water becomes a little muddied when you also have off-line marketing programs, seasonal variations in your business, or an existing online sales flow when starting a new PPC program. Fortunately, a number of tools can help you measure your progress.

At the most basic level, you should set up and pay close attention to Google's conversion tracking tools. They are designed to help you determine the rate at which people who go to your site from an ad actually do something specific, like making a purchase or asking for more information or signing up for a mailing list. Capturing an online sale is obviously the best indication that your PPC investment is paying off. If you have a more complicated sales pipeline, one that includes both on- and offline marketing, determining the value of a click can be more difficult.

Google's tools can be accessed by going to the "Reporting and Tools" menu in your AdWords account and selecting "Conversions." There is a setup wizard that will guide you through the process. These tools will enable you to tell Google what the different types of "click" on your site are worth to you, making possible a more accurate calculation of ROI.

Many third-party analysis tools and analysis service providers in the market can also help you measure and analyze your site. Some can be quite extensive in the amount of data they collect, and they will have a fee structure that reflects this. For the typical business or professional practice, properly utilizing the basic Google tools will give you the data you need to make good business decisions.

3. <u>Set it and forget it.</u> For people who are not familiar with just how dynamic the search engines are and how frequently algorithms change, there is a temptation to identify some keywords and put a few ads out there, supposing that you'll continue to see good results. Even if you are making big bucks with PPC, you must relentlessly evaluate and adjust. It is fairly easy to do, it

carries very little risk, and doing so has a huge potential upside.

Here's the Rule: "If it ain't broke, don't fix it," does <u>not</u> apply to PPC!

Do you think that a big search engine like Google is reasonably stable? After all, they are the world's largest. In fact, in 2015, Google changed their algorithms three hundred times (that they told us about). That is more than once every business day of the year! Not all of these changes will have a direct effect on PPC, but certainly enough of them will that it behooves you to closely monitor your account results and be diligent about evaluating. The mantra, "test-track-change," is adopted by all successful PPC managers.

Setting up A/B tests of ad headlines, landing pages, call to action phrases, and every other aspect of your campaigns should be the rule, not the exception. (An A/B test measures the effect of changing one of the variables in an ad by running two ads that are identical except for the variable you are testing.) You should always be on the hunt for better keywords, better ads, and better ways to convert ad-clickers. Even a small improvement in sales can make all the difference if it tips you into a positive return, because then you can start spending big and amplify those returns.

Here again, Google offers some helpful tools. A "bid simulator" gives you an indication of how well a new keyword might work for you. The "campaign experiment" tool helps you divert a small portion of your budget to a parallel test, then shifting money over to it if it scores big, or terminating it if it flops. You might also try campaigns on Bing, Yahoo, and AOL.

Even after you have everything optimized and running smoothly and profitably, it is a good idea to take a step back every so often to see if there isn't a way to take things up to a higher level, or to adapt to the ever-changing conditions of the internet.

All of this might seem like a lot of work…because it is! On the other hand, a well-designed and maintained PPC campaign can be the single-largest source of new customers for your business.

4.   Poor Money Management. With traditional advertising channels like radio, the newspaper, or the Yellow Pages, it has always been difficult to know what is really producing revenue. Too often, budget decisions have been made based on what "feels right" or on the size of your main competitor's ad. That is a really bad way to budget for pay-per-click; you will almost certainly be throwing money away or passing up the opportunity to hit a home run.

Here's the Rule: If you're getting a positive return on investment, base your budget on that and nothing else!

Using the analysis tools, you should be able to calculate, with reasonable precision, the return on your PPC investment. The beauty of PPC is that it can be adjusted quickly. Little changes can provide big results. When you get great results and are making money, you know it is time to spend more. If you were earning two dollars for every dollar you spent, how many times would you repeat the behavior? Do this until you either can't handle or just don't want the extra business, or until the monthly cash outlay becomes so large that it threatens to cause cash flow problems. An AdWords account is quite flexible—you can pause it at anytime.

5. <u>Keyword Management</u>. A related concept to poor money management is poor keyword management. Since you must bid for keywords in an AdWords bid marketplace, if your keywords are not highly desired by other advertisers, you can get good ad placement for very little money. If you are a chiropractor in a competitive marketplace, or a home improvement service in an area with several other strong providers who have more money to invest, you might be spending bids of several hundred dollars per click on "hot keywords."

Here's the Rule: Find your best keywords through consistent research and constant testing.

Following are three ideas to try, to keep your keywords relevant and costs down.

First, go local. This is a growing trend that first became popular about eighteen months ago. What it means is that you append common search terms with your location—for example, "DUI Attorney Dallas" or "Plastic Surgeon Denver."

Second, focus on less-obvious keywords (ideally ones that reflect your business specialties and strengths). An example might be "chimney repair" for a roofing firm that does tuck-pointing, flashing, and cap replacement on chimneys. This kind of call will often lead to more business.

Third, use negative keywords. This strategy helps to ensure that your ad is only being shown to people who are searching for what you actually offer. It is a simple strategy, but we frequently find that very few campaign managers employ it. The potential cost of overlooking this strategy is in the thousands of dollars. Two simple examples will make this clear.

- You are a plumbing contractor, using AdWords to find new clients. Do you want your ad shown to someone looking for a job as a plumber? Of course not. Some good negative keywords for your campaigns would be "career, careers, roofing careers, and plumbing jobs." When searchers type these words or phrases in their search, Google would not show your ad.

- You have a dental practice that performs implants. Your research reveals that many searchers are looking for a different type of implant. A good negative keyword in your case would be "breast."

Get the idea? Implementing this one strategy could dramatically improve your ROI. Your AdWords account should be closely monitored to identify the words and phrases being used by potential clients. Once you have this data, it becomes a simple process of "in with the good" and "out with the bad."

Can I Hire Someone to Do This for Me? How Do I Do That?

Managing a PPC program with multiple campaigns and ad groups takes both time and expertise. It is a specialized enough task that many practice owners choose to outsource their PPC marketing. If that is something you want to explore, here are some tips for finding the right company.

1. Make sure that the firm you are using has the technical ability to manage your account. Many times, an ad agency will offer PPC management, but they turn your account over to outsource teams without knowing how to hire or manage the outsourcer. Often, the people who are actually doing the day-to-day monitoring and managing of your account are not in the United States. Another technique some firms use is to "macro-manage" accounts, meaning that your technical manager will make changes for accounts by grouping accounts rather than by making changes customized to your business—to them, you become a small fish in a big pond. Pick a management team with technical support that is big enough to be competitive, but small enough to manage your account like the VIP you are!

2. Google offers a comprehensive certification program for PPC account managers. It requires a candidate to complete a training program, to obtain continuing education each year, and to have experience managing individual accounts with a minimum monthly spend in excess of $10,000. Look for a manager who has made this level of commitment to their profession.

3. Ask for total transparency in reporting. You might not want a report each month that is so technically detailed it needs a translator (although one should be available if requested), but you should have basic metric information available to you upon request. This should include cost, impressions, cost-per-click, click-through rate, cost-per-conversion, and conversion rate. Some account managers will supply you with more detail on such issues as click fraud (an account manager watching this area in detail can request credits for invalid clicks) or a campaign-change history that will detail how much work is being done in your account. Some account managers set up accounts, and then put them on a computer-controlled "autopilot." The campaign-change history is a good way to make sure this is not happening with your account.

4. Before you start a paid advertising campaign, your account manager should do a discovery profile of your business. The more the manager knows about your business, the better that manager can customize your PPC account. Some basic questions they should be asking are:

- What is your value proposition?
- Who is your ideal customer?

- What times of the day, month, and year are you the busiest?
- What is the transaction value of a new customer? Lifetime value of a new customer? What are you willing to pay to acquire a customer?

5. A good account manager will help you set budget goals that are realistic for your company at this time. More importantly, they will work with you to use profits from prior campaigns to build a marketing budget that is based on these profits, and not draining working capital.

6. A good account manager will set realistic goals so that you will know if you are on target.

We began this chapter by pointing out how PPC advertising has become critical to being found in search engine results. We also indicated that, far too often, we see business owners who think about paid search engine advertising like an ad in the Yellow Pages—put it out there and wait to see what happens.

This is a costly error! Pay-per-click can be the single-largest source of new business for your company, and the highest return on advertising investment you make. However, this will be only if you take the time to carefully monitor and manage your account. Don't let yourself get so busy that you ignore your PPC account. It is better to pay a management fee for an effective and well-managed account than to save a few dollars doing it yourself... and then not doing it.

WHAT TO DO NOW:

1. Decide if pay-per-click is a marketing channel for your business. If yes, decide on the monthly investment you are willing to make in PPC advertising. It is not uncommon for the cost-per-click to be $35 or more, meaning that to get one hundred clicks in a month would be a $3,500 investment.

2. If your intended monthly spend is going to be $1,000 or more, then we strongly encourage you to hire an experienced manager. Even with a relatively small monthly investment, a qualified PPC account manager will pay for themselves, both in campaign results and in the time they save you.

It is common for a PPC manager to charge you a monthly fee plus a percentage of the ad spend. For smaller accounts, the percentage may not be charged. You will need to shop around, and use the criteria we suggested earlier to interview account managers. If you talk with one of the large companies offering PPC services, WordStream or BrightLocal, for example, pay close attention to their agreements and how they are going to manage your account. Will you have a specific person assigned as your point of contact, or will you be working with one of their "teams?"

3. If you choose to manage your PPC account "in house," you may find value in a report that you can download for free at this link:

http://0s4.com/r/T2SMVW

Our report will give you a series of detailed checklists to follow as you create and manage your account. This will help you maximize your return on PPC investment.

Gordon Van Wechel & Jennine Michael

Chapter Six

Real-Time Bidding—Pinpointing Your Target Market

The strategy that we are sharing in this chapter, "Real-Time Bidding" (RTB), may be a new marketing channel for you. It is technology that was "invented" in 2010, but only in the past eighteen to twenty-four months, has it become widely available to smaller, private businesses. Until the middle of 2014, the cost to acquire and manage the software necessary to conduct an RTB campaign was so prohibitive that only large, national corporations could afford it.

That has changed. As the owner of a professional practice working in a single metropolitan area, you can now access this technology, and design and deploy your own RTB campaigns. We use this effective strategy for our own business, as well as for our clients.

To help you understand the power of RTB and consider incorporating it into your practice marketing plan, this chapter will cover the following information.

- What is real-time bidding?
- What is data-targeted traffic?

- What are differences between real-time bidding and direct ad buying?
- What are myths or misconceptions about real-time bidding?
- How can I use real-time bidding as a marketing tool in my practice?

You may have already experienced one type of RTB— what we call "retargeting." Have you ever visited a website, and then seen banner ads for that company on your screen for the next few days as you surfed the web? If so, then you have been retargeted. A more in-depth discussion of retargeting is included as another chapter in this book, but in brief, here is what it looks like.

The initial site you visited has been programmed to retarget visitors. This is done by placing a "cookie" on your computer. If you leave the site without responding to a call to action (like buying something), then an ad for the company is automatically placed on other websites you visit. These ads can be programmed for how frequently that you see them (down to how many times per hour!), as well as for how long they will follow you. The ads are called "banner ads." They can be created in several standard sizes. If you eventually click on one of these banners, you will be taken back to the company's website, or more likely to a landing page that is reflective of your specific interest.

This is all a bit complicated; that is one reason why it is a relatively new industry. It takes tremendous bandwidth and processing power to manage the fifty billion banner impressions that occur each day. This computer power has only been available for the past four years. The RTB industry is growing geometrically. From a mere $396 million spent on advertising in 2010, the industry saw 2013 revenues of $3.35 billion! In 2014, this grew to $4.55 billion, and predictions for 2016 are for ad placements totaling as much as $7 billion. This is *extraordinary* growth. By way of comparison, it took television advertising more than forty years to achieve the advertising revenue that RTB has hit in just three years.

What is Real-Time Bidding?

Real-time bidding refers to the means by which ad inventory is bought and sold on a per-impression basis, using a programmatic instantaneous auction. It is similar to how the financial markets work for the buying and selling of stocks, bonds, and commodities.

The easiest way to describe RTB is as a "data-driven auction." What that means is that as an advertiser, you have identified the best prospects for your business, and you are going to bid at auction for the opportunity to place your advertisement in front of those prospects. You design a "clickable banner ad" that meets the requirements of the auction house and is approved for use. You create an account with one of the demand-side platforms (DSP) and fund the account with your advertising budget for that campaign. We will cover DSPs in greater detail later within this chapter.

When your ideal prospective client is online and visits a website that allows banner ads (several million sites!), there is an immediate auction conducted between the companies who are bidding for that customer. This auction takes place in the time it takes for the website to load onto their screen, approximately fifty milliseconds. If yours is the high bid, then your ad is displayed. Your account is charged one cent above the second-highest bid. That cost is not for the individual display of your banner ad, but it is calculated for a total of 1,000 impressions—your ad being displayed 1,000 times. This is referred to as a "data-driven auction," because you define the data for your ideal prospect so that only someone who fits your specific criteria is shown your ad.

Another way to understand how RTB works is to use an example relating to the stock market, Wall Street, and the network of stock brokers all across the country. You own a practice, Smith Family Dentistry, and want to sell stock in your company to the public. That transaction would fall under the Securities Exchange Act, so you are not permitted just to run an ad in the local paper and hand people a Smith Family Dentistry stock certificate in return for their cash. First, you must file a large amount of paperwork and have your stock approved for sale with the New York Stock Exchange (for the sake of example, we'll use the biggest venue). When your stock is accepted for sale, you can send your prospectus to stock brokers across the country so they know about it and can share the opportunity of your practice with their clients. Eventually, a buyer is found for shares of your stock, and a transaction is made.

Real-time bidding works in a similar way. Owners of websites, called "publishers," decide to offer ad space on their site. They inform the "Ad Exchange" of the availability of this inventory. Think of the Ad Exchange like the New York Stock Exchange. These publishers are large sites like the national television networks, Facebook, and the online *Wall Street Journal*. Your local television station has a website that allows advertising. So does your newspaper, in its online edition. Many company websites do, too. In fact, there are literally tens of thousands of sites on specific niche topics that make their owners a great deal of money by offering ad space to the Ad Exchange.

You are the advertiser, and you want to have your ads

placed on these sites. To do that, you cannot go directly to the Ad Exchange, but you must use a demand-side platform. A DSP functions like a stock broker: they take the ads you have created and get them approved by the Ad Exchange, create an account for you and enter your ads into auctions targeting prospective clients as you have defined them, and, when your bid wins, the DSP pays the Ad Exchange, who then pays the publisher.

How do you find a DSP? Alchemy Consulting is a demand-side platform, dealing with the Ad Exchange on behalf of our clients. Also, to be fair, at the end of this chapter we will give you links to other DSPs to evaluate.

What is Data-Targeted Traffic?

The more precisely you can define who your ideal prospect is, the more you can focus your advertising spend. That is the real advantage of RTB as a marketing channel—the ability for an advertiser to target precisely who their ad is placed in front of. You probably have a general awareness that there is a significant amount of data collected on each of us as individuals. Our buying habits can be tracked using the UPC code on everything we purchase, the websites we visit are logged by the search engines, and our credit cards and loyalty cards reveal much about who we are and what we enjoy.

What you may not be as aware of is that all of this data

is held in repositories, by companies the majority of us have never heard of. Most of us know of the credit reporting companies—Equifax and TransUnion, for example. However, do you know NexAge or Criteo? How about PulsePoint? Until we began investigating RTB as a possible service to our clients, we were not aware of these companies either. In fact, as a DSP, we can access twenty-nine separate databases that record (and then sell) personal and business information on anyone with a credit card or a computer.

It is more than a little astonishing how precisely you can target your advertising. Is your ideal patient a married woman in her thirties who has a child less than 18 months old, drives a Ford sedan, has a college degree, owns her home, and enjoys aerobics? You can choose to put your banner ad in front of that woman, but not her forty-seven-year-old neighbor!

That is the value of data-targeted traffic!

Data can be categorized into two segments: first-party and third-party. First-party data is what you personally know about your customers based on your experiences with them. Third-party data is all of the other criteria. RTB is based on third-party data, and that data can be organized into several "buckets," or targets, that you can choose to market through. They are:

1. <u>Retargeting</u>. As detailed previously, it is the simple act of dropping a cookie onto the computer of someone who visits your site and then offering them ads for a programmed period of time. Think of this as "internet stalking," and it will be obvious how it works.

It is great for someone who actually visits your company website. For those prospective clients that haven't or don't, or if you have a new site that is stuck on page nine of the search engine where no one can find it, that is when the other RTB targets become valuable.

2. <u>Geo-Targeting</u>. Just like it sounds, "Geo-Targeting" allows you to identify a specific geographic location and target everyone in that area, like an entire state or just a single zip code—your choice. You can choose specific neighborhoods within your city and make an offer just to the residents living in that part of town.

You are not limited to the United States. We can do a geo-targeted campaign in 240 countries, and in forty different languages. Such is the universal nature of the internet.

Geo-targeting is the RTB method most often used by local professional practices.

3. <u>Contextual Targeting</u>. This type of RTB is based on keywords, but not the keywords someone enters into

their browser to search for a website. In this case, the keywords are contained within the written text that is on the site. Another way to think of this type of targeting is a "semantic" search. Semantics provides the true page meaning beyond the keyword.

An example might be a website that provides stretching exercise suggestions for people with back pain. If you were a chiropractor setting up an RTB campaign and included "Contextual" as one of your targeting methods, your banner ad might appear on this website, as long as the other criteria you set were met.

4. <u>Site Targeting</u>. This allows you to reverse-engineer where your competitors' ads run and place yours on the same page. You choose sites based on keywords. Assuming a competitor's website accepts banners, you could even have your ad pop up on their site when a prospect is searching for the service you offer!

You can also utilize a "negative site" option that is much like the "negative keyword" strategy in pay-per-click advertising; *i.e.,* identify those sites that you never want your ad displayed on. For example, a dental supply company site is not a place prospective patients would likely visit, so you don't want to pay for advertising on that site.

5. <u>Search Targeting</u>. Another powerful tool, search

targeting, allows you to display your ad based on the keywords that someone enters in. There are 750 categories that you can choose from. You can also submit a custom keyword list to the Ad Exchange for approval if your monthly ad spend is at least $2,000.

6. <u>Audience Targeting</u>. This method allows you, over time, to select a custom audience. The example we used earlier of a married woman in her thirties with a young child, etc. is the result of this type of targeted search. It is a strategy that is often used in high-end retail, like automobile or jewelry sales, but is not common for a professional practice.

What Are the Differences between Real-Time Bidding and Direct Ad Buying?

Purchasing blocks of banner ads is not new. In fact, it was one of the earliest ways to monetize internet real estate, going back to the late 1990s. As a small business owner, running online display ad campaigns can be a highly profitable marketing channel, one you may have tried yourself.

How is buying a block of display ads different from setting up an RTB campaign? The ultimate result is the same: you are placing your ads on a website somewhere. However, the process that an advertiser must follow to reach that end goal is very different, depending on the approach, and each has its pros and cons. Following is a comparison of some of the characteristics of traditional, direct banner-ad buys and RTB, to help you understand which approach may be best for your practice.

1. Targeting: Websites vs. Audiences

The fundamental difference between direct buys and RTB is the shift from buying ad impressions in bulk (direct), to auctioning each impression off individually to the highest bidder (RTB).

With direct buys, you are essentially buying impressions in bulk in order to have your ads seen in a specific context (*e.g.*, on ESPN.com). You have the ability to filter the audience that sees your ads with targeting rules such as geography or browser type, but still, you are ultimately targeting your ads to a specific website.

This works well for "brand" advertisers who are willing to pay premium prices to secure such inventory. Brands are also afforded more freedom on the creative level when working directly with publishers. Rich media formats, page takeovers, and other types of custom brand integrations are currently only possible with direct buys. The average professional practice typically does not have tens of thousands of dollars per month available to create brand awareness.

With RTB, each impression is profiled and evaluated in milliseconds during the auction process (while a page loads). You can target ad viewers at a demographic, psychographic, and behavioral level. The essential difference is the reach of RTB, which enables you to display your ads across a wide array of sites, rather than on just one. This makes it possible to target audiences at scale.

Instead of being limited to buying ads on ESPN.com to reach your audience, RTB allows you to buy ads on (almost) any site that "sports fans" may visit. You also have the ability to take a more agile approach to campaign optimization, since each impression is being bought individually, allowing for more efficient performance and control.

Everyone wants exposure to the right audience, which is why RTB approach works well for almost all advertisers.

2. Supply: Guaranteed vs. Non-Guaranteed

Another fundamental difference between direct buys and RTB is the level of certainty that your ad campaigns will receive the volume you want or need.

With direct buys, you agree to buy a bundle of ad

inventory at a fixed cost per thousand impressions (CPM) that the publisher will deliver in the future. In that sense, the inventory is "guaranteed" or "reserved" for you. Barring any external issues, you will receive the impressions you agreed to purchase.

This works well for advertisers that have specific exposure goals and require a high level of certainty that campaigns will deliver. In exchange for paying a higher rate to the publisher, you receive the certainty of campaign volumes and avoid the naturally competitive landscape of RTB.

With real-time bidding, as the name implies, you are in an auction with a multitude of other advertisers, all bidding in real time, at different rates for each impression. In such a dynamic environment, the ad inventory is considered "non-guaranteed," due to the unpredictability of the marketplace.

When you don't know what other people are bidding, there is simply no guarantee that you will win the impression you bid on. Furthermore, guaranteed buys usually have priority over RTB. This means that if the demand for guaranteed inventory on a particular site increases, the supply available on RTB for that site correspondingly decreases.

As an aside, this is another instance where knowing the acquisition cost of a client or patient for your practice is so important. Let's consider a fictitious dental practice as an example. Based on analyzing the other marketing channels, you know that it costs an average of $87.50 to acquire a new patient. Further, you know that the typical patient stays with your practice for fifty-seven months and spends $2,350 over that time.

Assuming that the CPM for ads to grow your dental practice in your local market averages $6.19, the natural tendency would be to bid $6.51 or something "just higher" than what seems to be the market. However, because you know that each new patient you can bring in averages $2,350 in revenue to the practice, a better approach is to set your bid at $35 or $50 or even $100. Why? As noted earlier, when you "win the bid" in an RTB auction, you only pay one cent over the second-place bid. If everyone else is bidding $6.20, you will win the bid and pay $6.21, even though you were willing to pay $35 or more. If you focus on the potential lifetime value of the patient in this example, logically you would be willing to pay far more than $100 to secure that $2,350 in revenue. It may seem counterintuitive to overbid, but this strategy will help you win more auctions and drive more traffic to your landing pages.

3. Workflow: Manual vs. Programmatic

Another difference between direct buys and RTB is the workflow of launching campaigns.

For the most part, direct buys consist of a manual process that involves hours of human effort in planning and execution. The process requires reaching out and making initial contact with the publisher's sales team, negotiating and planning the "insertion order" (a contract outlining the terms of the ad campaign), emailing ad tags back and forth, and so on—all in preparation to launch.

The publisher ultimately controls the flow of the campaigns using their ad server, which means that there is a natural delay when it comes to campaign control and reporting. This asynchronous process is not only prone to miscommunication and human error, but it also requires hours of human time on something that could be handled instantaneously with a programmatic solution.

In contrast, RTB is a primarily programmatic process, driven more by user interfaces and algorithms and less by phone calls, emails, and contracts. There are still manual elements (such as ad quality review, tech support, and billing), but nothing close to what is necessary when dealing directly with publishers—let alone a group of them. As a result of the programmatic process, more of the campaign components are real-time (*i.e.,* nearly instantaneous) in nature, from controlling the flow of campaigns, to reporting and optimization.

To be clear, even though RTB is a programmatic channel, that does not mean direct buys won't eventually enjoy a programmatic future. There are several ad-tech vendors in the marketplace giving publishers the ability to offer programmatic access to inventory on a guaranteed basis, all while maintaining control over pricing and ad quality. These technologies have yet to reach critical mass, so for the time being, we categorize direct buys in the "manual" workflow category.

4. Pricing: CPM vs. eCPM

Another primary difference between direct buys and RTB is the method by which inventory is priced. This difference stems from the fact that with direct buys, you are buying impressions in bulk, whereas with RTB, you are bidding on individual impressions separately.

Direct buys are almost always priced in fixed CPM rates, where the inventory is sold in bulk and all impressions are essentially priced the same (*i.e.,* $10 CPM, or $10 per thousand ad views). This pricing model has been the standard since the inception of the banner ad, and it doesn't look like it will be going anywhere in the near future.

With RTB, each impression is auctioned off. Since each impression is priced individually (and since a cost-per-impression metric would be wildly impractical to advertisers from a reporting perspective), the *de facto* metric for RTB pricing is *effective* CPM or eCPM.

Another way of thinking about how these two pricing models differ is by using an analogy like apples. Buying ad inventory directly from publishers is like buying giant bushels of apples. You pay a fixed price for each batch, and receive various levels of quality within the bunch.

With RTB, however, you are essentially bidding for each apple (impression) based on its individual characteristics. This means that you still end up with 1,000 apples at the end of the day, but the overall cost for the batch will be a dynamic value derived from all the individual prices you paid for each—hence the term, *effective* CPM.

5. Accessibility: Barriers to Entry

The final difference we want to point out between direct buys and RTB is the accessibility of each approach. Given the "traditional" nature of direct buys, they typically have much higher barriers to getting started, compared to RTB.

The first barrier faced by marketers or purchasers performing direct buys is the sizable ad spend minimums required by most publishers to get started. In general, you can expect a commitment of at least $5,000-$10,000 for a direct buy of guaranteed inventory.

On much smaller sites, you can get away with paying flat rates of a few hundred dollars. For larger publishers with attractive inventory, you won't receive any attention unless your budget is in the five- to six-figure range. For many small- to medium-sized local practices, this can be a non-starter.

As opposed to direct site buys or buys through large ad networks, which have higher barriers for marketers to get started, buying RTB inventory through a DSP (depending on the one you choose) has a much lower barrier in terms of financial commitment and operational management. Also, obtaining an ad server is not necessary, since DSPs provide the ad-serving and publisher integrations on your behalf. For a local business or professional practice, there is far more control and far less friction in the media-buying process within a programmatic RTB environment.

What is the bottom line? While buying ad inventory directly can be inefficient (not only from a price perspective, but also operationally), it does provide a number of benefits which can make these hurdles palatable to larger advertisers. Real-time bidding overcomes these pricing and operational problems, but introduces its own: guaranteed volume. For the business owner working in a local market, direct buy of banner advertising is not practical, whereas RTB can be a valuable source of new leads, at a price point far lower than what one might be paying a leads company.

Myths and Misconceptions about Real-Time Bidding

As with any emerging technology, there are bound to be myths and inaccuracies that circulate, often due to misunderstandings. Even if there is a hint of truth to them, often they can misrepresent reality by presenting exceptions as rules. Following are four common myths that we have come across in discussions about real-time bidding with prospective clients, as well as with other consultants.

1. The RTB Market Contains Only Low-Quality Inventory

There have been cases where suspect "publishers" have supplied the RTB ecosystem with questionable inventory. What this means is that the purchaser cannot accurately see where their ads have run. There may also be automated bots that produce false clicks, skewing the performance statistics.

In the last two years, this issue virtually has been eliminated, as most supply-side platforms (SSPs) and demand-side platforms actively work to remove such inventory from the marketplace. Low-quality inventory benefits nobody in the long run, which is why most vendors make an active effort to remove it altogether. Such inventory is definitely the exception and not the rule.

Fact: *Inventory from some of the largest publishers in the world is sold via RTB.*

2. You Don't Know Where Your Ads Are Running

Knowing where your ads are running is referred to as the "transparency" of your RTB spend. How much transparency you get depends on two things: your DSP and the inventory sources.

Fact: *RTB is one of the most transparent ways to buy media.*

As far as DSPs go, reporting varies by vendor. Some platforms may only report campaign-level statistics, with very little insight as to where your ads are actually showing up. Such lack of transparency cannot be attributed to RTB in general, but instead to the specific vendor.

For example, at our company, Alchemy Consulting, our software is configured to provide maximum transparency on multiple levels including: campaign-level, individual domain-level, placement level, and even to the creative level (each unique ad). This enables us to constantly be A/B testing on behalf of our clients, as well as providing them with accurate reporting on their monthly investment.

3. RTB Only Works When You Apply Cookie Data

The fundamental innovation of RTB is that every ad impression is auctioned off and evaluated by advertisers in milliseconds before being delivered. This has allowed advertisers to focus on buying audiences, using cookie data, as opposed to simply buying inventory from specific publishers.

Fact: *Running campaigns using cookie data for targeting is only one way to approach RTB.*

Some people have assumed that RTB is *only* made for buying audiences using cookie data. Having good first-party data for retargeting purposes is extremely powerful and performs very well in general, yet there are many other targeting tactics that don't rely on cookie data, but rather on other metadata associated with impressions.

Many advertisers achieve success with RTB the old-fashioned way—targeting specific publishers. One of the challenges with using data is achieving scale. By targeting specific publishers, you can effectively reach a target audience at scale, in a contextually relevant environment.

As a corollary, many people also believe that targeting specific publishers (or websites) isn't possible with RTB. Perhaps this is a problem with how initial DSP vendors chose to design their platforms, but it is more than possible to approach RTB campaigns in a way that is publisher-centric, rather than audience-centric.

Some DSPs focus solely on audience-based campaigns that require cookie data to function, while others offer advertisers the choice of either targeting audiences or specific websites. Using our company again as an example, as a DSP, we offer each of the targeting options that we described earlier. While most of our clients only use geo-targeting, some will occasionally layer contextual or site-targeting along with "geo" to refine their ad focus. We have the flexibility to design the campaigns you want.

4. Getting Started with RTB Requires a Large Budget

Since we offer service as a DSP, it pains me to read comments from marketers that believe RTB is only available to large advertisers with big budgets. That may have been the case in the early days of RTB, but that has not been the case for the past two years.

Fact: *The budget required to get started with RTB depends on the chosen vendor.*

Real-time bidding technology has revolutionized the way a large portion of display advertising is bought and sold. From a marketer's perspective, display advertising can now produce results like never before. However, the power and efficiency of RTB was initially only available to big brands and agencies.

As the industry has evolved, DSP vendors have evolved along with it, giving access to this world-class technology to advertisers of all sizes. When you think about RTB, know that it's accessible to advertisers of practically any budget.

How to Use Real-Time Bidding as a Marketing Tool in Your Practice

A question we are often asked is, "Should I do pay-per-click advertising or real-time bidding?" We always respond that that is the wrong question. A better series of questions would include:

- What is my marketing budget?
- How are my competitors advertising?
- Do I have someone on my team that can track campaign statistics and adjust my PPC and/or RTB campaigns as needed?

It isn't necessarily either/or, and it may not be both/and. In some cases, you'll want to have an active PPC campaign because that is the best chance you have of getting your practice's name on the first page of the search engines. RTB cannot do that. On the other hand, you may have defined a section of the city in which you want to capture market share. An RTB/geo campaign is the most cost-effective strategy to do that, more so than direct mail or blanketing the neighborhood with flyers.

What do we suggest for how a local business or professional practice uses RTB? We like to test for a couple of months with a small starting budget, $500 - $750 per month. If there is an area in the local market where our client wants to gain share, we set up a geo-targeting campaign. The display ads, as well as the landing pages they connect to, specifically discuss and refer to that part of town, giving the impression that our client is significantly active there.

In a highly competitive market, we also like to incorporate some site targeting, helping our clients identify what sites are attracting their ideal customer and advertising on them. Of course, we set up retargeting on their company website as well.

RTB advertising costs are rarely above $10 CPM. This means that a modest $500 budget can generate a great deal of activity.

RTB does produce a lot of data (much like PPC). If you are running several campaigns with multiple ad variables being tested, just the task of evaluating all the input can be a significant time commitment. For example, you can specify if your ad appears "above the fold" on the viewer's screen, how often an ad is displayed to an individual prospect, which landing page an ad connects to, and many other adjustments.

WHAT TO DO NOW:

1. Spend some time thinking about the questions asked in this chapter. Also, evaluate the other marketing you are now doing and its cost. Is RTB right for your practice at this time?

2. As you look for a DSP provider, here are some questions to ask:

a. Do you set up all the campaign and ad groups?

b. Will you do A/B testing of the ads and landing pages?

c. Who provides the creatives? Does this include both ads and landing pages?

d. What reports do you provide showing results for analysis?

e. What is the minimum monthly ad spend you require? What is your management fee?

3. Several demand-side platform companies to investigate are:

a. www.SiteScout.com/RTB

b. www.Criteo.com

c. www.Progmechs.com

d. www.TheExchangeLab.com

As with many of the marketing channels you might consider for your practice, an important factor to weigh is the amount of your personal time that is required for proper management and review. One of the advantages of RTB is that you can have your DSP handle all facets of the program. If you choose a DSP with a high degree of transparency in their reporting, you can implement an effective marketing program with very little of your time required once the initial setup is complete.

CONCLUSION

This chapter has far more detail than is probably of interest to you, but such is the nature of a new technology like RTB. It is a dynamic strategy that is still being refined.

The bottom line is that for most practices, a pay-per-click program supplemented with a basic retargeting campaign will provide "page one" search-engine exposure for your practice, with an appropriate level of additional exposure to site visitors. If you currently are, or now are building, a regional practice with multiple locations, then it may be time to consider an RTB campaign. A demand-side platform company can help you with that evaluation.

Chapter Seven

Video Marketing—Putting the World's #2 Search Engine to Work for You

Not too many years ago, if you thought about doing "video marketing," your only option was to produce and broadcast television commercials. While expensive, for many practice owners it was the best way to get prospective clients calling. Local cable advertising rates and video production costs have dropped, and still, this can be a powerful business-growth strategy for your company.

Some good news: you no longer have to hire an ad agency and expensive camera crews to produce top-quality marketing videos. In fact, with a smart phone and a little creativity, you can create dynamic marketing pieces that will inform, teach, engage, and amuse people. You no longer need to buy a package of airtime from your local cable provider, because now you can "broadcast" your videos on YouTube, Vimeo, Dailymotion, Hulu, and at least a dozen other video websites.

We want to demonstrate the importance and simplicity of video marketing for your practice, by covering the following areas:

- Startling facts showing why you need video marketing
- Types of videos to shoot
- How to get started producing quality videos for your practice
- How to set up a YouTube channel
- Strategies for marketing your videos

Why You Need Video Marketing

If you have any doubts about video as a marketing tool for your company, you may be enlightened by these facts and sources, compiled in early 2016.

- 203.5 million Americans watched 49.7 billion online content videos in August 2015. (ComScore)
- By the end of 2016, 90 percent of all web traffic will be video-based. (Cisco)
- Online video users are expected to double, to 1.5 billion, by the end of 2016. (Cisco)
- 52 percent of consumers say that watching a video makes them more confident in online purchases. (Inovodo)
- 55 percent of marketers who use video in their email campaigns reported an increase in click-through rate. (eMarketer)

- Globally, online video traffic will be 55 percent of all Internet traffic in 2016. (Cisco)
- Real-time video sharing will increase in 2016 with micro-video apps like Vine and Instagram video. (Forbes.com)
- 76 percent of marketers plan to add video to their sites, making it a higher priority than Facebook, Twitter, and blog integration. (Social Media Examiner)
- Videos on landing pages increased conversions by 86 percent. (WebDAM)
- More than one billion unique users visit YouTube each month, spending more than four billion hours watching videos. (YouTube)

Evidently, the question is no longer, "Do I need any videos to market my business?" The question should be, "How can I quickly and easily incorporate video into my practice marketing?"

Video? What Do I Do That Should Be on a Video?

You may be surprised to learn that much of what you do in your practice is worth being the subject of a short video. When many prospects are searching for a professional service, they frequently don't know what to ask. They might have heard horror stories about consumers who purchased a product, only to find that it didn't perform as advertised and then the seller disappeared. Most prospective clients want to find someone they feel they can trust to do a good job at a fair price, who will stand behind their service. The purpose of your video marketing is to let them get to know you, your team, and the quality of work you do.

Video is far more compelling than anything written that you can put on your website to facilitate this "know-like-trust" process. Some ideas for types of videos you might consider are:

1. Testimonials. Perhaps the most powerful marketing you can do is a short video with a client. These are quite simple to shoot, and they require almost no preparation. Here are some tips:

- An ideal length is forty-five to sixty seconds. This gives you enough time to ask no more than two questions and let the client respond.
- Lighting is important; avoid shooting in a room with fluorescent tubes. Ideally, you have a large window, perhaps in the lobby area or conference room, and can use the natural light available that day. Make sure not to position your people directly in front of the window so that the bright daylight is behind them; their faces will be difficult

to distinguish. Have the window at a ninety-degree angle to your subject.

- People are generally more comfortable in front of a camera when they are seated. You want to position your camera so that your subject's head down to the lower-middle portion of their chest is in the frame.

- Professional photographers have a phrase: "fill the frame." What they mean is to make the subject of the video, your client, almost all that is seen. Do not show a lot of wall space behind or table in front of them. Use the telephoto capability of the camera lens to "fill the frame" with your client.

- There are two ways to stage these videos, and creating a library that is a mixture of both is best. One method is to have one of your team members sit with the client(s), look to the camera and introduce them, ask one or two questions, then say thank you and finish. It is a very quick conversation, where the speakers are looking at each other and not into the camera once the introduction is made.

- The second method is to show only the client(s) in the shot, letting them introduce themselves, and then mentioning one or two things they especially appreciated about your company, team, and the work you did. You will prompt your client with the subjects before they start, but there is not someone directly asking them questions—it is their "candid" impressions. In this situation, they will be looking into the camera.

The questions and subjects we want to address are the "hot buttons" in the minds of prospective clients of your practice who will be watching. For example:

- Understanding the legal process and the way your firm helped
- Having representation at a tax audit, should one occur
- Getting good value for the investment made, and their satisfaction with the results (these are great questions for an orthodontist, cosmetic dentist, plastic surgeon, etc.)
- Working with your staff—quick response time, questions answered to their satisfaction, someone to help when you are not immediately available

2. Owner/Personality. This type of video features the owner of the practice. In some cases, an associate is used if he/she is more comfortable in front of the camera. No matter who you decide to use, it is important that the majority of your videos feature that person. They become the "face" of your company to the community. Again, some tips:

- These can be a little longer, depending on the subject matter. One to two minutes is a good length, unless you are demonstrating something that takes longer and is interesting to the potential viewer.

- Focus on subjects that will have meaning to someone looking for the services you offer. Do not shoot platitude-filled "commercials" about how you are the "best in town." It is fine to ask for their business, but give them a compelling reason to take the next step in the sales process with you.

- Feature other members of the team, especially as you develop a good-sized library of videos. For example, Mary in accounting is having her tenth anniversary with the firm this month, so film a short video introducing Mary and acknowledging her long service. This type of video will show people a human side of your practice.

  Some of the videos should be shot "in the office" and others, "in the studio." "In the studio" refers to a more formal background and lighting, like a portrait photographer would use. Proper advance planning will result in a library of videos that are meaningful to a prospect and which generate interest in your company.

3. <u>Demonstration videos</u>. Some professional practices offer products for sale. This video genre allows you to demonstrate how to use your product properly, or to

show potential issues a customer might face in the future as they use it. These videos are powerful generators of trust, and they do a great job of establishing you as an expert who is willing to share your knowledge. Some subject ideas:

- Tips for doing routine maintenance on the product you sell
- Product comparisons—be careful how you talk about your competitors' products!
- "Questions You Should Be Asking"—a great way for professionals to share expertise and educate potential clients
- Advanced ways to use what you sell

3a. <u>Animated Demonstration Videos</u>. Some demonstrations, particularly medical procedures, do not lend themselves to an actual "live" video. In that case, you would use one of the animated methods of production; these include 'Animoto,' 'Claymation,' and 'white board' videos. This introduction-to-video chapter will not go into detail on these techniques, but you can learn more by doing a Google search on each term. You might also find producers to help you by going to a website like www.Fiverr.com and entering "video production" into the search bar.

Hopefully, you now recognize that it is much easier to

come up with good subjects than you might have thought. Next, we will cover how to convert these ideas into top-quality videos

How to Get Started Producing Quality Videos for Your Business

When I talk with clients about video, they immediately assume they will need a lot of expensive equipment or will have to hire a production specialist. That is not the case anymore! Producing quality videos that show your company in a positive light requires only two things: basic equipment and a video plan.

You most likely already have the most important piece—the camera. If you have a relatively current smart phone, either an iPhone or an Android, you already have a camera that will give you quality, raw-video footage. Some people believe that one format is better than another, but we have found it hard to tell the difference between the finished video shot by either type, so whichever brand you own, you can feel confident using it.

As you begin to produce more video content, you may want to add some additional equipment. If you are going to create video in a room in your office, you will want a "green-screen" background—a solid color that you stand in front of when shooting the video. The neutral color will help your viewer focus on the subject of the video—you or the props you are demonstrating. Using very simple video production software (you probably already own some), it is an easy matter to superimpose your video over another background, like outdoors or in an office, by replacing the green-screen with a digital image.

A photographer's supply company will sell a fabric green-screen and the rack system to support it, but it is not necessary to purchase a professional-grade system. You can buy sheets of fabric and create your own, or, even simpler, buy a gallon of dinosaur-green paint and paint one wall. If you go this route, make sure it is a smooth wall, not textured, or you will not be able to light it easily.

A tripod to hold your phone/camera steady when shooting is important. Since your phone is lightweight, you don't need to invest in a heavy, professional-style tripod. Adapters that will connect the phone to a tripod can be found online or at tech stores.

For indoor shooting, controlling the light is important. You want to eliminate shadows cast by the subject against the background. You can go to a photographer's supply company and buy studio lights. Alien Bees is a company that manufactures very inexpensive but accurate studio lighting; we use them in our indoor studio. Again, you don't need to go to that level; great video can be produced using halogen shop lights from Home Depot or Lowes for less than $50. You will have to experiment with distance from the subject, since these do not have the light-intensity adjustments of regular studio lights.

Most important is sound quality. Your viewers will overlook average video quality, but if they have to struggle to hear what is being said they will click away in seconds. Invest some money in a good-quality wireless microphone. You can expect to pay around $125 for a system that will sync into your phone/camera. Do not try to skip this expense; whether you do most of your videos indoors or outside, good audio quality is critical.

A video-editing software program will be necessary for any "studio"-style videos you produce. If you use a Windows-based computer, then Windows Movie Maker is already loaded and ready to use. For Mac users, iMovie is your included program. Both are reasonably intuitive, with good help features.

Another option are programs produced by TechSmith. They offer a free program, Jing, which can do screen-capture videos of up to five minutes. For a more versatile (and complicated) solution, consider their Camtasia product. It is a complete video-editing platform that gives you total control over the finished product. You can upload video files from your phone for editing or create longer screen captures. We use this program in our office to produce webinars. The retail cost for Camtasia is about $250.

That is it. With these equipment basics, you are ready to be the Steven Spielberg for your company. However, to produce quality videos that accurately represent the good name of your company, you need more than just equipment. You'll also need a plan to create engaging videos that will hold the interest of your prospective clients. Here are some tips for how to do that:

1. Quality videos don't happen by accident—they are created with pre-production planning. The following components are a must:

- Shot list. Write down the different shots you want to include in your video. It may only be one or two for a short video, but plan them ahead of time.
- Story board. Make a simple sketch of any complex shots or transitions between shots. This is especially important if you're shooting at a location you are not familiar with.
- Prop list, per scene. A professional-looking finished product will be the result if you have everything ready and on-hand before starting the camera.

- B-roll. Additional footage will make your story come to life when it is time to edit. Some examples might include showing the exterior of your office building, or you walking around your office with people and activity in the background as you answer common questions.

2. **Be clear, and give a reason to stick around.** Make sure viewers know in the first five to ten seconds exactly why they should keep watching. Tell them, and show them the benefits they will receive from watching your video. Even for a short, forty-five to ninety-second video, use an attention-getting headline as you begin. People have very short attention spans when sitting in front of their computers.

3. **Be Energetic.** People who demonstrate passion and energy on camera are more likely to hold a viewer's attention than one who is monotone and dull. Watching a stand-up comedian will demonstrate how energy affects an audience.

Try speaking a bit louder than normal, and be a little more animated with your body language. Don't mumble. Look at the camera when appropriate, at the work you are demonstrating, and then back at the camera.

All this might feel strange, but it can create a more engaging video. It may take a little practice, but it is worth the time.

4. Post production. Once you have shot your video footage, what do you do with it? In some cases, like testimonials from customers, the footage is ready to go without any post-production work. Other times, you will want to load the .mp4 file into your editing software and make adjustments as needed.

If you decide to make video an important part of your company marketing, then you will want to have an "intro" and an "outro" created. An intro is a short, ten-second-or-less, clip that "brands" your company and your channel. An outro is another clip that typically shows your company name, phone number, and website address. Every video you produce should have the intro and outro added as a part of your post-production work.

Once your videos are created and produced, the next step is to upload them to your channel on the Internet's key video sites.

How to Create Your YouTube Channel

Producing a library of marketing videos is the first step, but you need a place for prospects to find and watch them. Enter YouTube, Vimeo, Dailymotion, Hulu, and a host of other websites that are designed to display video. The best way to make your videos available, while also enhancing your company brand, is to create a channel on these sites. We will cover specifics for YouTube, but the process is similar with the other sites.

How many sites do you need? Really, just one: YouTube. It is the second-largest search engine in the world, based on number of searches conducted. Recent statistics indicate that YouTube controls almost 85 percent of the online video marketplace. The value in creating your own channel and posting your videos to one or two other sites is that the search engine spiders crawl them, and there is page-rank value in being found on multiple sites. The video department at Alchemy uses several software programs for video-posting of our clients' videos on an average of ninety sites. This is more than required for displaying the videos to potential clients, but we also create back links to our clients' primary websites as a part of our process.

Creating a YouTube channel is an easy process, and you should be able to complete it in less than a half-hour. A Google search for "how to create a YouTube channel for my business" should help you find the most recent instructions. The process changes fairly often, especially as Google continues to integrate their various tools and programs. (You may be aware that Google owns YouTube.) As of early 2016, the steps are as follows (it is a very good idea to check for updates):

- Create a new Google gmail account and verify it. Verification is normally by telephone; it is not required in all cases, but be prepared to follow their steps if asked. If you already have a gmail account but have never created an associated YouTube account, you can use your existing gmail account.
- Click on "continue to YouTube," and you will be taken to a screen where you can set up the channel.
- In the right-hand corner, you will see an icon that looks like a person. Clicking on that will open a box with an option for "Creator Studio." Click it, and you'll see a message asking you to "Create a Channel."
- Input the name for your channel. You can use your own name or a business name. Type in the name you want, click the "agree" box, then click "Done."
- You will be taken back to a YouTube page asking how you want to use YouTube. Select the gmail address you are using, and the system will take you to your YouTube channel page.

- If you click on the "My Channel" option on the page left, you'll be able to customize your channel—adding an artistic background image, completing the "About" section describing your channel, and other features.
- Now you're done--you have a channel where you can upload your videos.

A word of caution: always research the most current steps before starting to create any new property with Google. In almost all cases, you will find a YouTube video that someone has made guiding you through the process. Look for the most recent videos and watch them.

Strategies for Marketing Your Videos

Some best practices for using your video channel as a marketing tool follow.

1. **How should I organize my video content?** Instead of presenting your videos in a single, long list, group them into playlists by topic or theme. With a little navigation, viewers can more easily find videos that interest them.

2. **How often should I post videos?** Upload new videos as often as your schedule and budget allow, especially as

you are getting started. Once you have a library of a dozen or more in your channel, you might create a publishing schedule and then announce on your website and through social media every time you publish a new video.

3. **How do I customize my channel background?** When designing your YouTube channel, try to mirror your company's existing online look, including the color schemes and logos on your website. You can choose a background color for your channel, and then upload your background image. This congruence will help establish your brand in the local market.

4. **Should I upload commercials about my products and services?** People generally come to YouTube to be entertained, educated and informed, not to watch commercials. The idea is to put helpful, informative videos on YouTube that enhance your company's image without being overly promotional. However, it is good to have a call to action; that is one of the reasons to add an outro to every video.

5. **How should I describe and tag my videos?** Video descriptions are often overlooked, but they are an important part of optimizing your video for the search engines. You can use up to six hundred characters of

information about your video. The first two sentences are particularly important, and they should include the keywords that are most important for the video.

Use keyword-search terms in your video descriptions. For example, if you're posting an on-the-job video showing chimney repair, add keyword tags like "chimney," "chimney repair," "flashing" "chimney cap," and "roof repair." That way searchers can easily find it via search engines and YouTube search.

6. Should I allow comments on my videos? Allowing people to comment on your videos should encourage them to share their experiences with your brand, and it shows that you are open to feedback. You can automatically display comments, display them only after you've approved them, or keep them hidden. If you enable comments, you still have the option to delete any that are inappropriate or spammy.

Just like Facebook and other social media sites, the comments section is where you directly interact with and engage your community. If you allow comments, realize that it is important to respond in the most helpful and authentic way possible, which means someone in your practice is going to have to monitor your channel(s) regularly.

7. How should I promote my channel? Every time you upload a new video, share a direct link to it across all of your practice's social media networks. You can embed your YouTube videos and playlists in the website or blog for your practice.

You can also try building an audience for your videos with Google Adwords for video, which lets you create and manage video promotions on YouTube and elsewhere online. Google Adwords campaigns are cost-per-view (CPV). To set a CPV bid, you enter the highest price you want to pay. For example, if you think it's worth twenty-five cents for someone to watch your video, set that amount as your maximum CPV. Then, you pay only when people watch your video.

8. How can I measure my channel's success? YouTube offers a free, self-service viewership-analytics and reporting tool called YouTube Analytics. It tells you how many people watch your videos, how often, and how they discovered your videos.

YouTube Analytics also shows how many subscribers you have, as well as how many likes, dislikes, comments and shares each video has received. Tracking which videos are most popular, along with the precise moment people stop watching them, can help you learn which types of content resonate with your viewers.

WHAT TO DO NOW:

1. Decide to incorporate video into your marketing! No matter what else you do to promote your company, video is *that* important on today's Internet.

2. Plan your video campaigns.
   a. Who in your company has a smart phone?
   b. Do you have a place in your office to shoot indoor videos? What is needed to set it up properly? Who will get it done?
   c. What type(s) of videos do you want to have in your library? How many? By what date?
   d. Does someone on your team know how to use your post-production software? Assign learning this to two people so you always have a backup in case someone leaves.

3. Set video marketing goals.
   a. When will you have your first "customer testimonial" live video?
   b. When will your YouTube channel be ready for uploads?

4. Assign a team member to the organizational components of this task. Rarely will you, as the practice professional, have the time to follow-through on the setup tasks and ongoing monitoring of your video

marketing program. Put someone in charge; it doesn't have to be a full-time employee. With a bit of searching, you should be able to find a high school or community college student interested in video and looking for "real-world" experience.

CONCLUSION

A video library benefits your practice on so many levels! It is critical for developing the "know-like-trust" with prospective clients that is the goal of your marketing program. The addition of video content on one or more websites increases your Internet footprint, making it easier for prospects to find you. Client testimonials are powerful social proof for the quality of your work.

If you follow the steps we have suggested, you can be creating video for your practice in a matter of days.

Chapter Eight

Appreciation Marketing—Mining Past Customers for Referrals

The strategy we will share with you in this chapter is perhaps the easiest, and most cost-efficient, marketing program we have used. It is a technique that is based on two concepts, both so well-known that they are almost intuitive for a business owner:

1. it is less expensive to work with a past client or their referrals than it is to go out and acquire a new client or patient, and

2. people like to feel appreciated, and they will reward you with their referrals when you express gratitude for their business.

While we all know these ideas to be true, how many of us actually take the time to stay in contact with our past clients? Other than offering thanks as you finish working with them, what do you do to sustain the goodwill you first created by doing a great job for them?

When we ask these questions to our new clients, the answer is usually, "Well... nothing." Some mail a thank-you card, but not consistently to all customers. Others send an occasional email asking for referrals, but again, not very consistently. Most do nothing, focusing their advertising budget on finding the next patient.

That is a mistake, and we will show you a system that can help you automate the process of staying in touch with past clients and creating consistent, top-quality referrals from them.

First, let us share some statistics from the Direct Marketing Association (DMA). The DMA analyzed the methods that most businesses use to stay in contact with their clients, as well as the "open rate" of those efforts—that is, how many customers actually opened what they were sent (with no guarantee that they read it, just opened it). You may find the data surprising.

1. An email: 12-15% are opened.

2. An email sent to an "opt-in" list (like a quarterly newsletter): 35% are opened.

3. A letter in a business envelope: 45% open rate. (people sort their mail over the trashcan)

4. A greeting card envelope: 94%!!!

When someone receives what looks like a greeting card, the odds that they will open and look at it are more than double what can be expected from other means to communicate.

You are probably thinking something like, "Great, I've bought boxes of thank-you cards. They're sitting in a desk drawer because I'm too busy to sit down and write the message and get it into the mail." We have the same problem. Maybe you've tried what we used to do—have the sales team write thank-you cards to their own prospects and clients. That worked...for about two weeks!

Many years ago, we solved this problem for our business. A friend who owns an advertising agency introduced us to a company called Send Out Cards. It is an Internet-based company that prints a custom greeting card and mails it for you. These are not electronic cards that come in an email, but an actual printed card delivered by the U.S. mail. It is a service that is almost too good to be true, especially considering how inexpensive it is.

How the Send Out Cards (SOC) Platform Works

The basic details for this amazing system are as follows:

1. Send Out Cards is totally "cloud"-based. That means that once you have set up a customer account with the company, you can access your account from any

computer in the world, as long as you have an Internet connection.

2. You have two databases within your SOC account. One is a "contact manager" list of your clients, patients, prospects, and vendors...anyone you might want to send a card to. We each have family members and non-business friends in our contact managers. It is a very robust customer-relationship manager that allows you to keep notes on each person on your list and track specific dates for that person, as well as categorize them into different groups that you define. Your data is completely secure.

The second database is the "card manager." Here you will find over 15,000 professionally designed greeting cards in more than two hundred categories (by way of comparison, a typical Hallmark store has between 1,700 and 2,000 cards to choose from). What makes the SOC program unique is that you can design your own cards, specific to your company, and have them printed and sent. You can send one card or one thousand.

3. You have a choice of four different card sizes: a standard postcard, a two-panel card like you would buy at the store, a three-panel card (almost like a brochure), or an 8.2" x 11.5" "big card," for when you really want to create an impression.

There is an option to create a font that is your own handwriting, so you can send cards written just like you write. If your penmanship is less-than-stellar, you may want to have someone in your office create the font!

4. You pay for the cards you send by using "points." While the dollar value of a point varies, the most economical choice is to become what is called a preferred customer and purchase points at $0.39 each. When you send a card, the SOC system deducts the points from your account. A postcard costs one point ($0.39). A regular-sized greeting card is three points, a three-panel card is four points, and a "big card" is fifteen points. Postage costs are always in addition.

Even more amazing, included in the price, you can customize a card with your company logo or your own photos. Think about that. You can create a custom, one-off greeting card using the SOC online card-creation program, upload a photo and/or your logo, and add a message in your own handwriting. When you push the "Send Card" button, you're done!

Send Out Cards prints your card file, addresses the envelope, puts the card in, then seals, stamps, and takes it to the post office. All of this is done within twenty-four hours, for a cost of less than a dollar, plus postage. You never have to leave your desk. Since it is a cloud-based system, you can enter orders any time of day, any day of the week.

5. SOC also provides the option of sending a gift along with your card. The last time we looked, there were more than two hundred different gifts that could be sent. Quite a few of these are appropriate for a professional practice to send to patients, clients, and associates.

6. Finally, the best part: the campaign function. Essentially, this feature allows you to create a card one time then use it as often as you like, with each card being customized to the individual recipient. When you create a campaign, you can use an "insert name" function that automatically puts the name of each recipient in the right place on the card.

You also have the ability to create multi-card campaigns. In effect, you can "touch" past patients several times a year—automatically. Literally, you just set up the campaign one time and then let it run. We have clients who create their card marketing for the year in January, and then an office person takes over from there, adding new patients or prospects as needed throughout the year. Since cards are so inexpensive, you can contact your past clients quarterly for about $6 per year. In most cases, just one referral from one past client will pay for your entire program for the year!

How We Use the SOC System

Over past years, we have evolved to a very streamlined use of Send Out Cards in our own marketing. Here are some of the things we do:

- "Nice to meet you" card after any first-time contact with a potential client or referral source. These are typically sent after a networking meeting.
- "Thank you" for just about any reason. So few people actually say "thank you" these days, we like to stand out from the crowd, and this is a big part of that effort.
- Quarterly touch with all past clients. These are *not* "send us your referral" pleas. Our philosophy is to offer valuable business insights or interesting facts that make people stop and think for a moment. This keeps us "top of mind," and in a positive, constructive way.
- Personal use. For birthdays, anniversaries, congratulations, etc., these cards often accompany a gift.
- Holiday cards. We do not send Christmas cards; so many companies do that very few prospects really remember who sent them a card. We send a patriotic card on the 4th of July, and another card the week before Thanksgiving.

You Can "Test Drive" the SOC Platform

Following is an affiliate link that you can visit to explore the Send Out Cards program and send a card to yourself to test the system. There is no cost to you to do this. That link is:

www.SendOutCards.com/IMS

As you look through the site, you'll see that Send Out Cards uses the Network Marketing business model to grow their company. You can use the system as a customer without becoming a distributor or "joining" anything. As a Preferred Customer, you can buy cards and gifts at the same cost as a distributor. We would recommend this option if you decide to incorporate appreciation marketing into your company program.

WHAT TO DO NOW:

1. Follow the link above and look through the SOC system. A video tutorial is available that will introduce you to the various parts of the platform. Send a card to yourself. Pay particular attention to the campaign function—it is a great tool for business users.

2. To learn some additional ways you might use Send Out Cards in your business, we have written a report entitled, "29 Ways to Grow Your Business Using Appreciation Marketing." You can download the report

using the link below.

https://goo.gl/SrcdTF

If you decide you want to utilize the SOC system, and you become a customer through our Affiliate Link, we'll send you three of the campaigns we use. Once you have your customer number from Send Out Cards, send us an email with that number, and we'll transfer the campaigns to your account. Gordon's email address is Gordon@TheAlchemyConsultingGroup.com.

3. Whether you decide to use SOC or to buy cards and manage your own system, we encourage you to begin an appreciation marketing campaign.

Appreciation marketing is overlooked too often by busy business owners, yet it can pay huge dividends in both goodwill and referrals.

The value of adding an appreciation marketing component to your marketing plan we believe can best be described by an observation from the late Maya Angelou. She noted, "I've learned that people will forget what you said, people will forget what you did, but people will never forget how you made them feel."

Chapter Nine

Total Market Takeover®—Done For You

If you'd like to have Alchemy Consulting working as your "in house" marketing team, implementing the Total Market Takeover® on your behalf, we will do that. Let us share with you some of the basics about how we work, and then you can decide if you'd like to discuss a business relationship.

At Alchemy, we believe that being honest and transparent about our working styles, our policies and procedures, and our expectations of ourselves and our clients is the best course of action. We do this before we start working with a client, and for some, Alchemy is not the right marketing agency for their practice at that time. That's okay; it is better to figure it out sooner than later, after we've both invested in the relationship.

Our Core Principles

Alchemy sells marketing and business-growth expertise, not time billed by the hour. To help us do our best work for you, we need all decision-makers to be involved from the start of the project. We are not in the business of talking people into things. Our goal is to help us both evaluate a mutual fit and develop the best solution for your business, currently and into the future.

What Our Ideal Client Looks Like

You are looking for a partner in growing your business, not a vendor who sells "off the shelf" answers. You don't expect an overnight fix or miracle, but a long-term, sustainable marketing solution that solves problems for you. You are honest with us, and yourself, about your needs and realistic budget. You are willing to participate when we need your collaboration and input.

What You Can Expect from Alchemy

We will give you our honest opinions, even when we're fairly sure you may not like them. We will be diligent in keeping your project moving forward and maintaining schedules we've agreed to. That means that sometimes we will push you to get things done. We will show humility if we make a mistake—we're not perfect, nor do we expect you to be. Our normal work hours are from 8 a.m. to 5 p.m. MST, but we are flexible when needed. We are available to meet by phone, online, or in person. We use Zoom for online conferences. Our fees and terms are specified per project or product. We always separate the cost of consulting from your "ad spend," and we will provide you with a monthly reconciliation of all ad-spend dollars. We do offer "packages" of congruent services to help our clients save money and make a faster impact in their market. These packages are detailed below.

What We Expect from Our Clients

We prefer a prompt response to our requests for information and approvals, so that we can keep your project a priority. We request that you honor deadlines. We presume that you have a clear understanding of what we provide, as defined in our agreement. We anticipate that you will pay our invoices promptly.

Service Packages

We know that for some clients, a single marketing strategy will generate the desired result and meet their capacity for new patients. Others are interested in a broader program, focusing more resources at business growth to achieve a faster outcome. To accommodate both, we have created several service packages that bundle congruent strategies.

We offer these packages at less than the cost of implementing the strategies individually. If you have read this book, the strategies will be familiar to you. Following is a quick overview of the three service packages.

<u>Silver Services Package</u>:   Maximizing Your Online Reputation

- Claim 30+ online citation sites for your company
- Create a private review page

- Market to past clients for reviews
- Provide video-based staff training center for reputation awareness
- Monitor review sites daily
- Produce, optimize, and syndicate one reputation video each month

<u>Gold Services Package</u>: Your "In House" Marketing Department

This is our best value for your investment, and our most popular program. It includes each of the Silver Services just described, *plus* the following strategies, implemented on a schedule that we work with you to determine. All of this is done for you, at far less than the cost of hiring an employee to manage these marketing strategies (assuming you could find one that was qualified!)

- Produce, optimize, and syndicate three "expert interview" videos yearly
- Get found online click-through/"dwell-time" strategy
- Create content for up to three URLs and fifteen keywords, up to five articles each month, creating powerful links to your website(s)

- Produce a webinar marketing storyboard, script, and an "evergreen" webinar targeted at one of your ideal client groups
- Design appreciation marketing campaigns and implement totally "done for you" service
- Implement media authority program: achieve citation by the four national networks

Platinum Services Package: Becoming a Market Leader in Your Community. In addition to *both* the Silver and Gold services, our Platinum clients receive:

- Create your business brand, crafting a consistent and trustworthy message
- Create quarterly press releases, sent through hundreds of news outlets
- Produce custom videos—we work with you to script five videos on subjects you choose, then shoot, produce, and syndicate them for you
- Create two additional evergreen webinars, targeted at different customer niches
- Generate guest-post articles for you in your business niche (six times yearly)

We also offer, on a limited basis, one additional program. **Total Market Takeover®** is our trademarked, "full service" marketing plan. It is available to no more than two businesses in a niche within a city. It includes every service described in the three previous programs, plus what we call "You-Everywhere-Now."

Using our unique "10x10" content-creation formula, we will work with you to produce a series of podcasts and videos, as well as a book written by the owner of your practice (we ghostwrite it for you). Content is distributed through multiple channels in your market area, making you the acknowledged expert in the industry.

Marketing Audit

Whether you choose an individual strategy or one of our service bundles, the first step in the process is to complete a "marketing audit." This is a snapshot of your current marketing practices, as well as your thoughts on growing your company. You can request a marketing audit form by sending an email to Gordon@TheAlchemyConsultingGroup.com, or download a copy from this link.

http://0s4.com/r/K4HGYR

Once you have returned the audit, our team will use the information to formulate a strategic plan for your practice. We'll set up an online or telephone conference with you to discuss the plan and answer your questions.

The Bottom Line

Over the past thirteen years, we have developed an understanding of the challenges faced by professional practices, and an expertise in helping you grow your business. Let's have a conversation about working together. Our toll-free number is (877) 978-2110.

Chapter Ten

The Eleven Most-Asked Questions about Working with the Alchemy Consulting Group

1. Who is The Alchemy Consulting Group?

Alchemy is a strategic marketing and business-growth consulting firm started in 2010 by Jennine Michael and Gordon Van Wechel. It is an outgrowth of a consulting practice that Gordon first began in 2003. Between them, Jennine and Gordon have over sixty years of combined, hands-on entrepreneurial experience, each building and selling several businesses of their own. All of Alchemy's associate consultants are experienced business owners, as well. That means we know what it's like to work eighty hours per week and to "wear all the hats" in the business.

Unlike most ad agencies or more-traditional consulting firms, Alchemy has created a menu of services; we call them "modules." These have been designed to provide our clients with specific solutions to business-growth challenges, regardless of how long they might have been in business. Whether you are the owner of a new business just starting out, or you have an established company looking to expand, we can offer tools and strategies to help you take the next step. The benefit to you is that we don't expect you to fit into our "marketing mold." We are able to help you evaluate exactly what you need, and can afford, at this time in your business.

2. Why Do I Even Need a Consultant?

Every great sports star, business person, and superstar is surrounded by coaches and advisors. As the world of business moves faster and becomes more competitive, it can be difficult to keep up with the changes in your own industry, in addition to the innovations in marketing and management. Having a business-growth consultant is no longer a luxury; it has become a necessity.

In all honesty, you know that can be almost impossible to get an objective answer from yourself. That is not to say that you cannot survive in business without a consultant, but it is almost impossible to thrive.

A consultant can see the forest for the trees. A consultant will compel you to focus on the game, making you run more laps than you feel like. A consultant will tell it like it really is. A consultant will give you small pointers. A consultant will listen, and understand your pain. A consultant will help you remember the dreams you had when going into business...and help you get back on track to achieving them.

3. What is the First Step?

We'll ask you to complete our marketing audit. This is a series of questions— most of them are simple yes/no answers, but there are several questions that will require a more detailed response. The purpose of the audit is to help you pinpoint current areas of strength in your marketing, and to help identify those aspects of your plan that could use additional work. People participating in this exercise commonly experience many ideas and much excitement about what can be done to bring in more clients and profits. The audit will also prompt some questions about specific marketing tactics and how to implement them.

Once you have returned your audit, we will schedule a time to meet together. This typically is a sixty- to ninety-minute conversation, where we help you dig deeper into the level at which your practice is performing today, and where you'd like it to be in twelve months. It is also an opportunity for you to get to know us a bit more, and to see if working together makes sense. At the end of the meeting, at your request, we will prepare a proposal detailing our recommendations specific to your practice, and the investment you will be making. You can then decide when you'd like to begin.

There is no charge for this initial meeting.

4. What Will You Do, and How Long Will it Take?

Just as every person is different, we believe each practice is different. The plan that we suggest for your practice will be based on the evaluation we make after reviewing your marketing audit and the conversation we have in the initial meeting. We cannot give you a *specific* idea of what we will do in your practice until we have designed your plan.

We can tell you that while about 80 percent of our strategic marketing focus today is online, we still incorporate traditional offline tools like direct mail and telephone marketing. We do this because they work. The particular mix of strategies for you will depend on your goals, current situation, budget, the competitive landscape, and personnel available to handle an influx of new clients.

Part of the marketing audit considers your current capacity—that is, how much more business can you handle well? It is of no value to your business to suddenly bring in thirty new clients when you only have the staff to serve five of them properly. We call this evaluating the "inside reality" of your company, and it is included in our modules.

Regarding how long a typical program might take, we like to make commitments in twelve-month increments.

We don't try to lock clients into a contract declaring that, but the plan we design for you will be based upon a year of implementation.

If you've been in business for more than a few months, you've already seen, and maybe even purchased, one or more so-called "quick fixes." Most consultants want you to believe that they can solve your business-growth problems in a few days. Our philosophy at Alchemy is that establishing a foundation for long-term success in your practice means not just scraping the surface with a few "Google secrets." We prefer to design a multi-channel marketing strategy that offers you controlled growth. That means implementing one or two modules initially, then, as they pay for themselves, adding more marketing. Over the course of a year, working together, we help you fully capitalize on current markets for your service and extend the reach of your practice into new areas.

5. How Do You Know This Will Work in My Industry Practice Niche?

It is simple, really. Our consultants are experts in sales, marketing, business development, management strategies, hiring key people, and evaluation of markets—just to name a few of their competencies. With more than 250 business-building tactics in our arsenal, you will quickly see how effective and powerful our modules are.

Add to this the fact that we have consulted with more than 300 companies in over fifty business categories, and you can see that, very likely, we have worked in a practice that is the same or very similar to yours.

6. How Much Time and Money Will This Cost Me?

For the first couple of months, your involvement in the processes will require more time. That might be to review copy or collateral materials, train your team in a new sales system, or attend regularly scheduled update meetings you'll have with one of our team members. The actual implementation of tactics—what we call the "back-office fulfillment" duties—are all done by one of our groups of specialists. If part of your program calls for a revision of your website, the actual work will be done by our web builders. If you are doing a real-time bidding program, then another of our teams will handle the daily details of that marketing channel for you.

As to the financial investment...well, nothing! That is, if you look at it from the same perspective as we do—the difference between a cost and an investment. Everything we propose for your company is a true investment in your future. Not only will you create great results in your practice, but you'll learn more than just marketing strategies. Working with our consultants will give you an education from experienced entrepreneurs that you could never get in school, and this is knowledge that you can repeat over and over.

So you don't think we're dodging the question, here is a range. We have clients who invest as little as $500 monthly, and others who spend $10,000 a month. How much you spend will depend on your practice, budget, short- and long-term growth goals, and how aggressively you want to pursue them.

7. Are There Any Guarantees?

Will all of your business goals be met by working with us? Maybe, or maybe not. We will never promise a specific result, nor can we guarantee that any of your goals will become a reality. The bottom line is that we are your consultants; it is still your practice, and it is up to you and your team to take the sales opportunities we bring you and convert those prospects to clients and eventually to raving fans of your business.

Only *you* can be fully accountable for your success. We guarantee to give you the best service we can and the benefit of all our experience and proven business-growth strategies, and to encourage and even cajole you to reach for your goals. At the end of the day, though, it is your practice.

Here is the guarantee that we do offer. When we work with you to design a strategic plan, we will define clear goals that should be achieved within the first four months of working together. If they have not been achieved in that time period, then we will continue to work with you at no charge until those goals have been met.

8. You're Based in Another City—How Does That Work?

You may have read Thomas Friedman's book from a few years ago called *The World Is Flat*. His point was that with the communication tools available today, business has truly become international. Even the shoe store down the street can have an E-commerce website or a store on eBay and sell to the whole world. Our business is living proof of that new reality: 80 percent of our clients live in other cities or states. We regularly supply them with reports and updates via email and hold progress-review conversations using phone or Skype.

Occasionally, a client will want us to be at their location for a specific purpose, but generally that is an expense that you do not need to incur.

9. Do You Just Help with My Marketing?

While our primary focus is on marketing and business-growth strategies, we will help you in other areas, too.

For example, part of our reputation marketing module includes a training program to help your staff become more adept at customer service. We mentioned earlier the concept of the inside reality of your company; we will help you identify operations within your business that can be improved.

We strongly believe in systems. The more you can implement systems in your practice, the better you can run your practice instead of having it run you!

10. When is the Best Time to Get Started?

Yesterday. Truly.

Right now, today—before you take another marketing step, waste another dollar, lose another sale, or work another sixty-hour week.

Far too many business people "wait and see." They confuse activity with accomplishment, thinking that working harder will make it all better. Remember, what you know got you to where you are. To get to where you want to go, you've got to make some changes and, most likely, learn something new.

There is no time like the present to get started on your dreams and goals.

11. How Do I Start?

Call us toll-free at 877-978-2110, and ask for a marketing audit. You'll be connected with one of our consultants who will help you get started. We will set up a time for an interview so we can learn about your practice. Then, we will work with you to create a plan that helps you achieve your goals, on a timeline that is affordable and makes sense for your practice.

At the beginning, this may seem like a big job, but with an Alchemy consultant, you'll have someone guiding you each step of the way.

What Our Clients Say...

"In brief...the ideas Alchemy implemented paid for their fee within the first month!"

Ronald Guenther, President, Consolidated Mutual Mortgage

"While we have been fortunate to grow quickly in the past two years, Alchemy Consulting pointed out some areas where that growth was not being managed correctly. One was in making our install crews aware of their importance in developing our reputation in the community. (Alchemy) helped us put in a training program, as well as get great reviews from past homeowners and put them online. Now we are getting regular bid appointments due to our reputation."

Ted Bachmann, Owner, First Choice Roofing

"I have worked with several marketing companies over the last eleven years. My experience has been that they are focused on selling me "their program" and not sensitive to our company needs and direction. Working with Alchemy was so refreshing because they spent several hours asking questions, analyzing our marketing materials, talking with some of our customers; in short, they really worked to understand my business. When they did come back to me with recommendations, they were based on what was needed for our business and not some off-the-shelf program."

Robert Potter, Academy Technical Services

"Thank you again for turning me on to this incredible, easy to use, effective system of communication! I have seen tangible results in production, as well as positive feedback on every level."

Debra Stowers, Sotheby's International Realty

"Alchemy helped us really dig into the characteristics that make our firm unique, what they call the "inside reality." Then their team of outstanding copywriters and web designers gave us a strategic marketing plan that helps us tell that story to our prospective clients."

Richard Olsen, Hunter Associates, CPA

"After several years of frustration with paying for search engine advertising and never being sure of an ROI, we retained the Alchemy Group to manage our pay-per-click program. Within two months, we could document a significant increase in clicks and, more importantly, better quality prospects who really fit our practice model."

Clarence Oakley, Partner, Copeland Associates, Attorneys

"Before we started doing business with Alchemy Consulting, I'm not sure we ever got one new lead from the Internet. Now we have a website that is giving us new leads almost every day, and automated follow-up systems that nurture a relationship with prospects before we ever meet them!"

Lindsey Sheba, Metro Roofing

"Last month, we had a booth at a trade show. The Alchemy team designed the materials to give to people in the booth, but also a follow-up card to send to new contacts right from the show. They helped us develop a system for organizing all of these new contacts into specific funnels so we sent only the most relevant information to each visitor.

"Two things happened. First, almost every prospect complimented us on our quick and accurate follow-up with them. Second, we have been able to set appointments with seventeen companies that we had never been able to talk with before! The difference was our strategic planning going into the trade show, and the execution of that plan organized by the Alchemy team."

John Baca, Vice-President Operations, Uveon Funding Group

"The Alchemy Consultants work like I do. What I mean by that is they use checklists and timelines, document what the deliverables are, and provide regular progress reports. Plus they talk like business people and not "designers." When they say marketing is science and not art, they really mean it."

Allen Morton, Attorney

"A challenge for our marketing team has been to identify cold market prospects and introduce them to our firm. We especially appreciate your assistance in analyzing our past customer database, and then creating a target-100 group. Setting up a "drip campaign," as you call it, to these prospects has resulted in over twenty opportunities to provide a proposal to companies we had not worked with in the past. A huge success!"

Adrian Wheeler, Vice-President Marketing, Carousel Creative Services

ABOUT THE AUTHORS

Gordon Van Wechel is an entrepreneur who has built three national companies, each in a different industry. Previously, he has written five books, numerous articles and training manuals, and he has been cited by all four of the major television networks as an expert in business marketing.

Gordon is a frequent speaker to business groups, and he teaches a marketing class to new business owners on behalf of the Service Corps of Retired Executives (SCORE) division of the Small Business Administration.

In addition to his own enterprises, he has travelled extensively in Asia, Africa, and the Middle East on behalf of several non-governmental organizations. His work there has focused on micro-enterprise programs that, to date, have resulted in the creation of over five hundred successful businesses, seventeen village schools, and numerous community development projects.

He is currently the President of The Alchemy Consulting Group, a marketing strategy and business-growth firm based in Albuquerque, New Mexico.

Jennine Michael, CEO of The Alchemy Consulting Group, is a New Mexico native and a graduate of UNM who has a strong background in business. Formerly, she was affiliated with Lincoln National, focused on business insurance, until joining Merrill Lynch as an investment broker. Jennine is also the founder of Chef Michael Cakes, a specialty and wedding cake boutique bakery. Her focus in business has always been on building and retaining client relationships.

She managed her late husband's dental practice, coming to know the unique business qualities and needs of a professional practice. After his death, she learned how to sell and transfer a professional practice, and how important it is to plan properly for a transition of that nature.

The Alchemy Consulting Group is the result of accumulated wisdom, business best practices, and proprietary strategies, all to focus on one thing— providing clients with profitable new customers and patients. At Alchemy, success is measured by just one thing: results.

It is Jennine's passion—and the mission of The Alchemy Consulting Group—to help hard-working professionals grow their practices in order to provide a quality lifestyle for their families and into retirement.